Zlatko Bezhovski

Online Business Startup Guide

(Part 1)

ISBN: 9798718337822

Independently published

Biizly.com

Online Business Startup Guide
(Part 1)

Contents:

""The true entrepreneur is a doer, not a dreamer. The critical ingredient is getting off your butt and doing something. Not tomorrow. Not next week. But today."
– Nolan Bushnell

Everything you need to start a simple business online is time, few bucks ($50), internet connection and a laptop. Yes, it's that simple to start, but remember, there is no guarantee that you will be successful. The most important factors to succeed are your **long-term devotion and your willingness to learn** new things (as you go).

BEFORE YOU START

Before you start reading and implementing this Guide, bear these things in your mind:

1. You can be successful online!
Everyone can accomplish success online if he/she tries hard enough. The internet is a huge marketplace. There are billions of people out there and they need information, advice, help, services and products. You can find your role in that world, provide value for those people and make money out of that. You just have to stick to your dreams and be determined to succeed.

2. Don't get easily overwhelmed!
Anything new can appear to be overwhelming at first, but don't worry; you will quickly get the hang of things. If you already have experience and tech knowledge that's great, but it is definitely not a requirement. You will learn everything you need by doing. Sometimes, you may need assistance for some tasks or issues, but there are easy ways to get help.

3. Success doesn't come overnight!
Don't be afraid to make mistakes or fail. Don't quit easily. Everything you learn or do now, and every step you take will contribute towards your success in the future. Rome was not built in a day; your business won't be either. Even if you fail at your fist journey, you will gather valuable knowledge and experience for your next.

ABOUT THE GUIDE

The main goal of this Guide is to provide a simple flow of **all necessary information and resources for starting and running a web business**. The information and instructions placed in the guide are free, understandable and implementable even for beginners.

Another intention of the guide is **to motivate and push the wannabe online entrepreneurs to start their first online business**. Don't be afraid of failure, most of the entrepreneurs don't succeed on their first attempt. Therefore, don't just read, but start doing the things, step by step. You will learn everything you need as you go. At some points our guide might get detailed, but you can always skip the main text and go to the summary of each topic and glance the most important aspects you should know.

When using this guide, there are three (3) different **approaches**;
- The first (1) one is to read the entire guide, afterwards start your business and mark your progress using the startup checklist (biizly.com/cl). The checklist will then help you easily find explanations and essential resources in the guide wherever you need them.
- The second (2) **approach (that we recommend)** is to read and implement the guide step by step while you use the checklist alongside. This way you will be able to learn how to start an online business by doing (as you go) without reading everything upfront, what can be demotivating, can take too much time or can be easily neglected or forgotten later when you start your journey.
- The third (3) approach is to start with the Online business startup checklist and use the guide as a reference in the areas where you will need information and more detailed knowledge. The third approach will help you **quick-start your online business,** if that's what you are looking for.

So, unless you prefer the first approach, download the complementary Quick Startup Checklist right now at <u>biizly.com/cl</u> . There you can mark-up you progress right away since our recommendation is to start making the first steps today.

Good luck, and may your endeavors meet your expectations!

Step 1: Understanding the Online Business Basics

 "Learning by doing is the only way I know how to learn" – *Tony Fadell*

Key Points in Step 1:

- Starting a business online could be very simple.
- You don't need (tons of) money to start. You can even go with $0, but our advice is to start with at least $50 for a domain name and hosting
- You don't require any special skills; you will learn anything you need as you go.
- You can also outsource most of the operational tasks at affordable rates.
- The web environment empowers you with variety of business models and online revenue sources that you can harvest.
- Start building a personal brand and online authority even before you consider starting a business

Introduction

One of the biggest obstacles when starting a business is the fear of the unknown and many times, the misconceptions. Forget any misconceptions you have and put the fears aside because the concept of making money online is really simple.

To start a web business you don't need to read tons of books or get endless lectures and certainly, there is no need to pay some online "gurus" to teach you do so, especially at this stage, where you still don't know what the possibilities and your preferences are. You also don't need tons of money to invest since you could start online even with zero dollars ($0). Anyhow, at this point you need to get acquainted with some basic concepts of the online business environment.

Our guide aims to provide all necessary information and resources for your (first) online business journey in a simple meaner and a straightforward way. Our idea is to guide you through the process, step by step, teaching you the things in the time when you need them. We encourage you to start your online business as soon as possible but let's get acquainted with the basics first.

1.1. The Concept of Making Money Online with a Website

"The longer you're not taking action the more money you're losing."
– Carrie Wilkerson

At a Glance:

The Concept of the Online Business is simple:

1. Define your offering > 2. Start a website > 3. Attract visitors > 4. Earn revenue

The concept for earning money online with a legitimate business model is very simple. Some aspects of the process may not be that easy to implement, but if you manage to **put all the pieces in place**, you can eventually build a successful online business.

The process of making money with a web business consists of three major phases: *Defining your **offering**, Starting a **website** and Attracting **visitors**.* If you efficiently go through these phases and manage them appropriately, you can easily achieve your goals and *Earn **revenue**.*

The concept of making money online with a website:

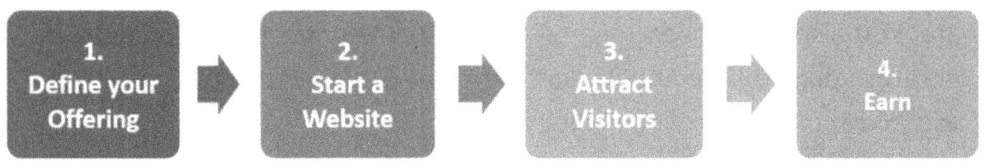

The concept of any web business presented in phases like this is simplified, but it shows **the big picture**. This Guide, more or less, follows this concept and will further elaborate the phases where we will go in more details and explanations.

Here, in order to clarify the concept, we will just shortly discus the phases:

DEFINE YOUR OFFERING

First thing you need to do, when starting a business, is to decide what you are going to offer to your potential customers. We use the term offering to describe a wide range of **products** (physical and digital), **services** and **information** you can offer to the internet users worldwide in order to satisfy their needs and demands.

Billions of internet users out there have interests, questions, problems, desires and needs, so your role will be to target one (or few of these) and solve them via your offering in a profitable way.

At this point, you should not worry what exactly you are going to offer because if you can't develop or **create your own products or services** you can always offer someone else's for a commission (via **online mediation**). You can also publish ads on your website and earn. In such cases, your **competitive advantage** should come prominent, not when you develop the product or service, but in the next two elements of the online business, especially in the third (Attracting visitors).

When deciding what to offer to your online customers, the most straight forward approach is to **follow your interests and/or your field of expertise**, but it's not the only way to go. Despite that, you can choose any field or any business idea you like, based on a **business opportunity** you discover or your **inner intuition**. In any case, you must have intention and determination to gain and **grow your knowledge/expertise in the field** or topic you choose.

Investigating the needs of the customers, finding the right ideas to pursue and defining your offering is something we discus in more details in Step 2 and in Step 4 in The Guide.

START A WEBSITE

After you decide what to offer to the internet users, you should start a website where you will place your offering.

Building and managing website these days is super **easy**. Often, not tech savvy people who want to start a business online, find this issue most frightening but believe it or not, this is usually the less challenging part. There are free **web tools** that will enable you to **set your website in 30 minutes** or less. The more challenging issues come when you need to enrich your site continuously with interesting and engaging content, what is part of the next phase.

In some cases, depending of your online business concept, you might need a custom solution for your website but fortunately, the most types of online business can go with standard websites that can be easily started and managed with free website builders like **WordPress**.

Starting and managing a website is something we discuss in Step 3 and Step 5 of the Guide.

ATTRACT VISITORS

Here comes **the biggest challenge** for every online business owner. The fight for the customers' attention on the net and their hard-earned money is vigorous. Attracting visitors to their sites can sometimes be challenging for experienced online marketers and established business too. However, you shouldn't worry ...much, since **there are many techniques and channels available online to bring visitors to your website**.

Besides the efforts to bring in the visitors, you should also strive to **keep their attention, earn their trust** and convert them to loyal customers on a long run. The process of attracting website visitors in order to earn online is challenging not because it is hard to do, but because there is competition, **it requires time, patience and some experience**.

You can define your offering very fast and you can change it /adopt it later if needed. You can also set your web site easily and enhance it gradually. When it comes to attracting visitors, you will need to put long term effort and time to create **engaging content**, build your following on the **social media**, earn good positions in **search engines**, build your list of **email subscribers**, find profitable **ways to advertise** and so on. However, if you master the skills for attracting and keeping the attention of the customers your road to online success is ensured regardless if you have or not own products and services.

We will discuss strategies and technique for attracting visitors in more details in Step 6.

EARN REVENUE

Earning revenue or making profits is the **desired outcome** of any business. The way you will generate income online depends on you offering, or more precisely, on the **revenue model** you select. You can sell products or services (own or someone else's) and earn **sales revenue**, you can recommend products and services and earn **commission,** or you can simply **publish ads** on your website and earn from that. (The revenue models are explained later in Step 1)

The potential of earning online is huge. **You success** will depend on many factors including your idea, your skills, the profitability of the industry/topic you get in, the level of competition etc, but, as mentioned before, the most important factors are your willingness to learn new things (as you go) and your long-term devotion.

***

To conclude, **in order to make money online you should first** *define your offering* **(products, services, information), then** *build a website* **where you will present the offering and at the end you should work to** *attract visitors* **to your website**. If you successfully manage to put in place all these aspects of your online business the visitors will recognize the value in your offering and will start generating income for you.

Summary:

- **The concept** of earning money with an online business is simple:
  1. Define you offering > 2. Start a website > 3. Attract visitors > 4. Earn
- **Define you offering:** Offer goods, services or information, in order to satisfy a need or solve a problem.
  – You don't need to have your own products or services; you could offer someone else's for a commission or publish ads to earn.
  – Approach 1 – follow your interests or field of expertise when deciding about your offering
  – Approach 2 – select any idea you believe will be a successful based on insights or intuition but become expert here.
- **Start a website:** It is easy to start and manage a website using free web systems (such WordPress) or other affordable options.
- **Attract visitors:** Not an easy task but doable. Many online strategies, techniques and channels are available for you to attract visitors.
- **Earn revenue:** Putting all important elements and phases in place can bring you profits. There are plenty of revenue sources and online business models you can implement.

Task:

- Start marking your progress in the Startup Checklist (biizly.com/cl)

In-depth readings (Search at Biizly.com):

Work from Home – The 3 Options.
Worthless Offers to Make Money Online
Turn Your Passion into Profitable Online Business
Make Your Online Business Successful in 7 Steps.

1.2. Required Resources and Skills to Start a Business Online

"Build your skills, not your resume." - Sheryl Sandberg

At a Glance:

Basic Requirements (Computer, Internet, Time, Willingness to learn new things as you go)

Initial finances ($0-$50+)

Essential Skills (To poses or outsource): Website management, Basic graphic editing, Content creation, Online marketing

Advanced skills (Not essential but handy): Product creation, Fast writing, Web coding, Programming, Advanced Graphic Design

People often assume that starting a business online requires experience, high level of technical knowledge and/or substantial amount of finances. In some cases, these might be true, but for many online business models, you just need a computer with an internet connection and determination (the needed finances could be neglectable).

The more knowledge and skills you have the better, but definitely, you don't need to know everything at the start. You will learn many new things as you go. You can also outsource (at affordable rates) the skills you don't possess or have no interest or time to learn or do yourself.

BASIC REQUIREMENTS FOR ONLINE BUSINESS STARTERS

You don't need much knowledge, experience and/or finances to start a business online, but the 4 listed requirements below are a must.

The **essential requirements** when starting an online business include:

- Computer and an Internet connection
- Basic Computer Literacy
- Time Devotion
- Willingness to learn new things (as you go)
- Small initial investment (domain + hosting)

The first two requirements are obvious (since you can read this), but if you don't have time to devote to your project and have no will to learn new things, starting a business online is definitely not for you.

Time devotion is very important when starting a business since you are the one that will have to set the foundation of the business and work the day to day tasks until you can afford employees and managers. This phase of the business may last for 3, 6, 9 months or even 1,2,3 years. Quitting your day job to start a business online might not be a good idea at the beginning but devoting 10 hour per week or at least 1 hour a day could be a good start. The good thing about the online businesses is that you can work on it in your spare time and still make success.

Since you want to run your own business, you should be **willing to learn new things** every day. This approach will help you start and run your online venture. In fact, there is no need to become expert in anything and everything, but you will need at least basic knowledge in several fields like website management, online marketing, outsourcing etc. what are super easy to acquire. The best thing when starting a business is that you can learn the stuff you need step-by-step as you work on your business, so you won't feel the burden and the "pain" of learning.

Here at Biizly.com, you can learn the basics for starting a business online, but also can go to more, in-depth knowledge, or find reliable sources to do so. In addition, most of the daily tasks required by any online business could be outsourced ... or done by the employees (instead of you as owner). In that case, you should at least learn how to set the strategic aspects of your business and know what to ask (and expect) from employees and/or freelancers. Anyway, giving job/tasks to others will additionally cost you money, what is unfavorable especially during the first stages of your new business.

As your business grows in revenue, you can focus more on the strategic aspects of your business and delegate the day to day activities to others.

INVESTMENT (INITIAL FINANCES)

Yes, you can start an online business without a dime. Anyway, if you are serious about your business you should register at least a domain name ($15/yearly) and acquire a reliable hosting plan that will cost you about $30 for the first 6 months. Another option (not highly recommended) is to get only the domain name and use some of the free blogging platforms like blogger.com.

Having this in mind, your **startup finances** could include:

- Initial investment (domain and hosting) $0 – $50
- Outsourcing (logo, web management, content writing, graphics etc.) $0 -$1000*
- Advertising cost (Google Ads, fb ads, etc.) $0 – $1000*
- Inventory (if selling physical goods) 0$ – $5000*

* The amounts are just an estimation to give you a clearer image where your initial investment could go.

As you can see, the biggest part of the investment could go for inventory, but the good news is that many online business models do not require any type of inventory. In addition, there are even business models for selling goods that don't require inventory of your own, like the affiliate model or the drop-ship model. In the drop-ship powered store, you will pay for the goods after you make the sale. After that, the provider will deliver the goods directly to the customer.

The two other "big" spendings could be for *Outsourcing* and for *Advertising* (if needed). Having that in mind, it is clear that more tasks you are able to do yourself, less you will pay to others and your initial investment will be smaller.

Regarding the advertisement costs, you should know that there are many online businesses that don't really need advertisement. Anyway, the advertisement should be considered as an essential part of the business since it can bring-in new visitors, can fortify the brand and can increase the revenue and profitability of the business. Our suggestion is to start your business relying on free methods of promotion and introduce paid advertising later. If you decide to advertise from the begging, experiment with small budgets first.

To conclude, to start a business online you will need around $50 as an initial investment. Your investment may increase a bit if you outsource some tasks like logo creation or content writing, but before you put your business on its feet and start generating some income you can do most of the needed task yourself. Later, after you sense the market and make some sales (or other type of revenue), you can start outsourcing, expanding your team, increase your investment and reinvest your earnings.

NEEDED SKILLS (ESSENTIAL AND ADVANCED)
(to possess, acquire or outsource)

Let's make it clear right away. You don't need to be tech savvy, a geek, or experienced online marketer to start and run a business online. The good news is that you will learn many new things by doing, as you work on your business. Not your current knowledge, but your willingness to learn new things and your determination will be crucial for your success.

By following this Guide you should gain the ability for the essential strategic thinking and you should be able to set the foundations of your future online business. You should also obtain informative and detailed knowledge about the needed day-to-day activities and operations to start and run your venture.

As mentioned before, the more skills you have (acquired) the better. You will be able to do more of the tasks yourself (you or your team members, if any), and you can do it in timely manner without paying for services. If there are some skills you don't know yet, don't stress. You will learn everything you need as you go. Everything else, that you are unable, unwilling, or have no interest or time to learn you can outsource to freelancers. (Employing other skilled workers during the starting stages of your business is often unnecessary and costly.)

Here is the list of **essential skills** (or sets of skills) that are needed to start and run an online business:
- Strategic thinking (Setting the foundations of your business)
- Website management (WordPress, Weebly, Magento or other)
- Basic graphic design (logo, image editing)
- Content creation (text, recordings (video or audio), infographics, etc.)
- Online Marketing (E-mail, SMM, SEO, Advertising)
- Outsourcing (finding freelancers to do the above-mentioned tasks)

Some of the mentioned skills/tasks are easy (to learn) and you can start doing them right away, for example the website management. Others, as the SEO (Search Engine Optimization), are more complex and require more time and experience, and some (as writing), might require some talent. If you develop expertise in any of these sets of skills, it may become your competitive advantage when running your business. You can also offer your expertise (as services) to other online business.

Finding other skilled freelancers to do the work, instead of you (outsourcing), seems as an easy task but it might get tricky. First of all, you need to know what to ask, then you should wisely choose who will do the tasks you need. Experienced and highly ranked freelancers may be expensive and/or busy to deliver on time or to communicate with you efficiently. On the other side, new and inexperienced freelancers, who are much more affordable, may deliver shabby job or not deliver at all.

At this point, it is very important that you develop sound strategic thinking ability, since you are here to start your online business. We hope that this guide will help you achieve that. After you decide to start your online business, the acquiring of the other skills will flow naturally.

Advanced skills in the areas mentioned above, are not necessary to start and run your online venture, but can help and ease the process since you can manage, enhance, improve, and fix your web site yourself on a higher level without engaging freelancers or you will be able to develop competitive services or products based on these skills.

Advanced skills that are not essential but could help your online startup include but are not limited to;

- – Web coding (HTML, CSS),
- – Web programming (PHP, ASP, Javascript)
- – Databases (MySQL MsSQL)
- – Programming, (Java, C#, C++, Python etc.)
- – Advanced Graphic Design,
- – Fast writing skills etc.

Additional and very important skills that can bring extra value to your business is the **ability to develop/create products or services**. Development of products and services is not simple since in some cases you will need in-depth knowledge and expertise in the field, in some investment and equipment, in some you will need talents and in other an entire team.

Types of products and services suitable for an online business may include but are not limited to:

- High quality content (articles, texts, books, e-books, videos, audios, photos etc.)
- Services (marketing, web management, online research, consulting etc.)
- Teaching and coaching (textual, recorded or live courses, classes etc.)
- Software (programs, apps, platforms, web services),
- Arts and crafts (paintings, sculptures, jewelry, home décor, gifts, pottery, clothes, etc.),
- Goods and commodities. (These may include handicrafts or manufactured goods)

The ability to create a competitive products or services can become your core business via internet and a competitive advantage. Anyway, **it is not necessary to develop your own products and services since you can also outsource them** (recommend and/or resell) trough affiliate partnership or from a drop-ship provider. Another option is to simply publish ads on your website and earn.

Regardless if you develop your products and services or you offer someone else's, you should acquire the essential skills mentioned above in order to set and run your online business.

Summary:

- You don't need some special skills or expertise to start a business online
- The most important to succeed are your determination and your will to learn new things as you go.

Basic Requirements to start a business online:

- o Time devotion (At least 1 hour a day)
- o Willingness to learn new things (as you go)
- o Initial investment of $0 to $50 (for Domain and Hosing)

Essential skills (to possess, acquire or outsource):
- o Website management,
- o Basic graphic editing,
- o Content writing,
- o Online marketing

Outsourcing:
- o Anything you cannot do or have no time to do (in-house), can be outsourced to freelancers or other companies at affordable rates.

Additional (Advanced) skills that might get handy but are not necessary:
- o Web coding (HTML, CSS),
- o Programming,
- o Advanced Graphic Design,
- o Fast content writing,
- o Product (or Service) development.

Task:

- Make a list of all needed resources and skills:
  - o What you possess? (In house)
  - o What to acquire? (Learn or Employ)
  - o What to outsource? (Hire Freelancers)

In-depth readings (Search at Biizly.com):
The single Biggest Mistake you can make when starting a Business Online
Want to be an Online Entrepreneur? Prepare first.
5 Important Skills to Start a Small Business Online
Website management: The Fastest Way to Start a Website
Content writing: 10 Tips for Writing an Appealing Article
Advanced Skills: PHP or ASP.net? What Should you Learn?
Outsourcing: Challenges when hiring freelancers.

1.3. Online Business Models and Revenue Sources

> *"Startups don't fail because they lack a product; they fail because they lack customers and a profitable business model." - Steve Blank*

At a Glance:

There is a wide range of online business models, revenue sources and combinations you can implement in order to make profits online

Online Revenue Sources:
Sales, Publishing Ads, Affiliate Commission, Subscriptions, Transaction Fees

Online Business Models:
Informative websites (Blogs), Online classes and coaching, Selling digital products, Online services, e-Shops, Interactive website, Market creators, etc.

There are many different types of online businesses you can start. The scope of business models and ways to make revenue online is wide. Some models are simple, some are more sophisticated and complex. Since the internet and the web environment are highly flexible, besides the basic online models and revenue sources described blow, there are also many other possible combinations.

Creating new models or new combinations that didn't existed before are not uncommon in the online world and discovering unique one can bring substantial profits for the innovators.

Anyway, you don't need to be extra creative or innovative to be successful. You can just follow a business model that works and be devoted and persistent.

ONLINE REVENUE SOURCES

Before we observe the online business models, first let's see where online money come from. The revenue sources, also known as revenue models, are integral part of the business model itself.

There are five basic types of revenue that you can generate online: 1. Sales, 2. Affiliate Commission, 3. Subscriptions, 4. Publishing Ads and 5. Transaction Fees.

Sales revenue

The most straightforward revenue source online is from direct sales. You can sell (almost) everything online. Besides physical goods (like crafts, jewelry, office supplies, clothing, electronics, supplements etc.) you can also sell digital products (music, videos, games, e-books, apps, software etc.). You can also sell information and services of different types. In order to sell directly to your customers, you have to provide services, generate information (or content) or possess the goods/products. If you provide the services or create the products yourself that's great, but you can also outsource them from suppliers. If you don't what to hold inventory you can supply your store trough drop-shippers who can send the goods directly to your customer after they make the purchase.

Affiliate commission

If you want to make a simpler online business and avoid creating an e-store, produce goods, buy from suppliers and/or keep inventory, you can decide to recommend products from other sellers for a commission. The affiliate commission can start form 2% for physical goods and can reach to incredible 80% (or more) for digital products like e-books, software, tutorials, video lesions etc. The range of affiliate products you can offer is wide. Almost any known brand, like Amazon, Target, Apple, offer their products through affiliate programs. There are also affiliate networks like CJ and ClickBank that bring together the business who offer their products via affiliate marketing and the business or the individuals who want to earn affiliate commission. The process for integrating the affiliate model in your business is very simple. You first apply for a program, after you get approved you copy-paste the links or embed the widgets in your site. Then you work to attract visitors to your site and motivate/send them to check the offer of the seller. If the visitors buy you get a commission.

For more details read our article: How to Start an Affiliate Marketing Business from Scratch (Biizly.com).

Subscriptions

If you manage to create a premium content, valuable (automated) web services or a software used as a service, you can generate income from subscriptions (weekly/monthly/yearly). In order to do so, you should have regular free content that will convince your user of the worth of your premium services, you should give a trial period, or you should already have built a loyal audience ready to pay for your offering . Since the internet users are used to have free content and free web services, you should create something very specific or with superior value, what is not easy to achieve if you are a beginner (unless you have already developed specific skills).

Publishing ads

The simplest way to generate income online is to publish ads on your site. The process of publishing ads is simplified by ad networks like Google's AdSense. In order to get approved for AdSense, you need to have original content on your site and have some history and inflow of daily visitors. After you copy-paste the Ads' code into your website you will have to focus on bringing and retaining substantial number of visitors there. This can be achieved by creating original, useful and engaging content that can include, articles, tutorials, tips, videos, podcasts etc. It is important to note that some topics/niches can bring more income per visitor than others. For example, having a blog for financial issues can generate higher ad revenue than a blog on human rights per visitor. Anyway, if you could bring more visitors to the human rights blog and generate more total income, that might be the right choice.

Transaction fees

The intermediaries that facilitate the interactions and transactions between two parties online can generate transaction fees. Usually these intermediaries are trusted and reputable business that have gradually built their brand, trust and users base. The transaction fee is charged when the deal is closed, when the payment is done, when the funds are transferred. The business that charge transaction fees include but are not limited to payment processors, auction sites, online markets, freelancing sites, advertising networks, affiliate networks, exchanges, accommodation services etc. If small and new business manage to bring users together and facilitate their transactions can also earn transaction fees.

ONLINE BUSINESS MODELS

A business model is a simplified picture of the reality and describes how a business creates value and how it generates income. The following basic online business models can give you a clear perspective of what business types you can start on the web:

1. **Informative websites** (blog, online magazine, news, reviews, online advice, niche sites etc.)
2. **Online classes and coaching.** (Video lessons, lectures, one-on-one tutoring or training)
3. **Selling digital products** (e-books, tutorials, podcasts, images, video content etc.)
4. **Online services** (personal services, business services etc.)
5. **e-Shops** (for any type of physical products)
6. **Interactive websites** (social media, online games, blogging platforms, forums)
7. **Market creators** (classified ads, auction sites, exchanges, online marketplaces or shopping malls, freelancing sites, etc.)
8. **Web services** (email, hosting, search, etc.)
9. **Transaction brokers** (payment processors, B2B intermediaries, advertising networks, etc.)
10. **Online businesses without own website**.

The list of the models is not definite since it lists the most common ones. The models can also be combined to create a blended one or a new model. For an example, you can combine an e-Shop with a blog or a social media site with a market creator. You can also combine e-shop of physical and digital products. If you combine web services with news and other information, you get something known as a portal like Yahoo or MSN.

Generally, the business model itself implies the revenue model too. For example; an e-store generates revenues from sales of goods, informational website that offer free access earn form ads or referrals, transaction brokers generate revenue from transaction fees and so on. Anyway, most of the business models can combine more than one revenue source. For example; an informative website can earn from ads and affiliate links simultaneously.

The given models, more or less, are listed according to the level of difficulty for implementation (form easiest to hardest, excluding the 10th model). Anyway, the difficulty depends from case to case. For example, it might be easier to create an e-shop than to develop own digital product for selling, or it might get very difficult to create informative website in areas where it's hard to obtain timely and reliable information. In addition, the 10th model (given as a bonus) can be considered as the easiest one since it excludes the need to build own website. The different business (sub) models without a website can be included in some of the other listed models (selling on eBay as e-shop, providing services on Upwork as online services model) but it's given as a separate one just to complete the picture of the online business a beginner can start.

Next, let's discuss the above-mentioned online business models from a perspective of a beginner in the online business world:

1. Informative Websites

> **Difficulty level**: 2 (on scale from 1 to 10), **Earning potential:** 2-5 (on scale from 1 to 10), **Main elements:** topic, website, content, promotion. **Revenue sources:** Main: Publishing Ads, Affiliate Commissions – Alternative: Subscriptions. **Key competences:** content creation/ acquisition, promotion.

This is the **easiest business model** type you can start online. Even if you plan to start online business of another type, first try with an informative website. If you succeed to attract visitors you may consider expanding to additional online models, for example an e-shop.

For this online business model, you just need a topic, a simple website and (enough) content. In addition, you will need to work on the promotion of the site and continuously add new appealing content in order to attract and keep the visitors.

The number and types of topics you can choose for your site is endless. You can start an informative site about fishing, diving, knitting, parenting, clubbing, crypto currencies and so on. You can choose wider topic like fashion or a narrow one like kids or even toddlers' fashion.

Since content is the cornerstone of this model make sure you create appealing content for the selected target audience. If you don't have talents for writing or you simply have no time or nerves, hire a freelancer. In any case, you will need interesting articles at least once a week.

Another important aspect of this business type (like in many others) is your ability to bring visitors to your site. There are many options how to promote your site but these set of skills is something you will learn gradually. We discuss the promotion later in the Guide.

The main revenue sources (after the visitors start to come in) for this model come from publishing ads and from affiliate links (If appropriate).

2. Online Classes and Coaching

> **Difficulty level**: 4, *Earning potential:* 3-8, *Main elements:* classes (and coaching), website, promotion. *Revenue sources:* sales of classes and one-on-one coaching. *Key competences:* skills to teach/coach.

Recorded online classes/lectures and one-on-one life coaching (or training) can be considered as two different business types but since they are complementary you can practice them together for the best results. If you don't have time to coach one-on-one, you can focus only on the recorded classes. Once you record them, they will be available 24/7 for your customers and you can easily scale your business (sell to a large number of clients) focusing mostly on the marketing. On the other side, the one-on-one coaching is more personal, you can focus on the client's specific needs and therefore you can charge premium rates. Anyway, since the one-on-one coaching takes most of your available time the potential for earning is limited.

It seems that this business type is not for everybody since it requires specific knowledge or skills and the ability to transfer (teach or present) the knowledge either directly to the client or as a recording or text lessons. Anyway, sometimes we are not aware of our skills and the need for them. For example, someone might be good at dating, other at traveling at low costs, some at parenting, some at gardening and so on. Many other people lack these skills or simply have no experience and therefore are ready to pay to learn. There is much evidence that this business model works even for unusual types of classes, like teaching a piano online for example.

Besides the ability to develop classes you will also need a website that will nurture related content in order to attract potential customers and motivate them to purchase your lectures or coaching. In addition, you will have to implement some methods and utilize different channels to bring visitors to your site.

3. Selling Digital Products

> **Difficulty level**: 2-4, **Earning potential:** 2-10, **Main elements:** product(s), website, squeeze pages, promotion, and affiliate network. **Revenue sources:** sales of digital product(s) or affiliate commission. **Key competences:** digital product development and/or promotion.

This business model has two faces, meaning two different approaches. One is to develop own digital product(s) and sell them for profits and the other is to resell/recommend someone else's products for a commission.

If you choose the first approach, you need to develop your own digital products (one or more). The digital products you can create include but are not limited to e-books, tutorials, guides, podcasts, videos, software, apps etc. Some of these products are easier to do, like e-books and others are very hard, like software and apps. The type of the digital products also determines the channels where you can promote them. For example: the apps are mostly sold via app stores like iTunes and Google Play. Therefore, here we will focus on products that anyone with the ability to write or present, can create like e-books, tutorials, guides, podcasts and videos.

In order to be successful when selling digital products, first thing to do is to identify a specific problem (or a need) that people have. Then you should offer a solution for that problem within the product (or series) of products you develop. Beside the product, you also have to create promotional materials like articles, banners, squeeze pages, promotional videos etc. If you don't already have a substantial followers base or subscribers to whom you can market and sell your products the best tactic is to join an affiliate network where other members could promote your product. Since these networks have large number of members, there is a huge earning potential in this method that is measured in 6 to 7 figures of income, in case your product is in high demand, is of high quality and has low competition.

The second approach in this model is to sell digital products developed by others, available in the affiliate networks and earn commissions for every sale. There are many digital products out there that you could promote and earn. The commission for such digital products can go up to 85% of their value, what could reach $100 or even more. The most attractive digital products you can promote include: fitness and weight loss programs, healthy cooking recipes, gardening, landscaping and more. There are also other exciting products you can promote like sporting tutorials, pet training, parenting, languages, software, investment guides, travel guides etc. After you decide which product(s) to promote the only thing you need to solve is where to promote them. The first choice, of course is to build a web site where you can nurture related content and work on it to bring visitors. Another option is to promote the products (with direct links) in social media, forums, chats or so.

In any case, when you try to sell digital products of the discussed types, you have to know that making cold sales (sending visitors directly to the products' selling page) is very hard. Instead, you should send them to warm-up articles or videos before sending them to the sales page. Since the consumers are mostly reluctant when buying such products, it is very handy to build a subscribers list around certain topic and warm-up the buying process with a series of free and useful emails.

4. Online Services

> **Difficulty level**: 2-5. **Earning potential:** 3-4. **Main elements:** service, website, promotion. **Revenue sources:** sales of services. **Key competences:** skills to deliver certain online services, promotion.

Under online services, we include all services that can be delivered via internet regardless if they are done in front of a computer or in the physical world. The difference between this model and the sales of digital products and classes is that here the service/product is not created upfront but upon order of a specific customer. In the other mentioned models, the service is developed with a target group in mind and prepared as a package (downloadable/accessible) for a large number of users. Here, the service is mostly custom and has no value or use for other clients. Therefore, this business model has limited earning potential. When you reach your own limits (full time engagement), you can hire others (employees or freelancers) to fulfill the orders, but your business can grow steadily, not exponential what might happen when selling ready digital products.

Services you may offer online include writing, customer services, internet marketing, translation, legal consulting, accounting, web management, software and web development, graphic design, audio and video production, data services, admin support and many more.

Since the online space is full in (almost) all of these areas, you have to pay a lot of attention to the promotion. So, besides creating a simple website where you present your services you should enrich your continent with related useful articles, give free services, guest post to other sites, promote locally, utilize social media and so on. Still, there is a long road until you reach substantial number of clients and become profitable. Having that in mind, one of the best advices when starting such online business is to offer your services at the freelancing networks where potential clients and freelancers meet. Starting at these networks is not easy too. The competition is worldwide and huge so the rates you can charge are low, especially if you are a newbie. Anyway, at these networks you can get customers faster than if you go with a website only. Since you can offer your services via freelancing networks and be successful it seems that a website is not quite necessary for this model, but, that's not quite true. With a website you can build your business on a long term, gain reputation, build a brand and acquire customers directly at you site avoiding the competition and the low rates.

5. e-Shops

> **Difficulty level**: 3-5. **Earning potential:** 3-5. **Main elements:** products (own or outsourced), website, e-commerce plugin, payment options, delivery and return system, promotion. **Revenue sources:** sales of goods. **Key competences:** skills to make (or outsource) competitive products, promotion.

The e-shops are probably the most obvious online business model. There are e-shops for (almost) everything. People can buy electronics, kitchenware, clothes, arts, toys, food, collectibles, music, video games and many more. We can roughly divide the e-shops in specialized and shops with wide assortment. The shops can also be local, national or global.

The space in this type of online businesses is dominated by the big players as Amazon, Walmart, Target, BestBuy and so on, but there is still room for smaller businesses if they follow the niche strategy. This means that if you want to start an e-shop, you have to select a specific niche (offer specific products to a narrow market segment). For example, instead of opening a biking store you can focus on biking accessories or only on biking helmets, or you can open, let's say, a specialized online store for spices.

Starting an e-shop is challenging for many reasons, especially if you are a newbie in the online business. Setting up your web store technically might not be that hard as finding the right and competitive products or as the efforts to reach your potential customers. Having that in mind, we recommend that you start a different online business type first, like an informative website, and later complement it with an e-store. Anyway, if you already have a brick and mortar business and you want to expand online, it will be less challenging than starting from scratch.

Whatever you decide to do, when you are opening an e-shop you have to offer something of greater value for your costumers than the competition. You can offer the lowest prices, the fastest delivery or extraordinary customer service. You could offer a specific product that is hard to find somewhere else. You can offer customizable products or customizable packaging. Another good strategy is to complement your products with a great content. For example, if you have e-store for spices you could tell their story and offer exciting recipes.

Since the competition is vigorous, another important aspect of your business would be the promotion of your store and the effort to turn your visitors to a first-time customers and after that to a lifelong loyal customers.

6. Interactive Websites (Web 2.0)

> **Difficulty level**: 5-8, **Earning potential:** 3-6, **Main elements:** website, interactive elements/plugins or online games, community. **Revenue sources:** ads, subscriptions, premium membership. **Key competences:** web development, promotion

To get access to more information >>> subscribe <<< to our mailing list.

7. Market creators

> **Difficulty level**: 5-9. **Earning potential:** 5-10. **Main elements:** website, back-end systems. **Revenue sources:** listings, transaction fees. **Key competences:** web development, promotion.

To get access to more information >>> subscribe <<< to our mailing list.

8. Web services

Difficulty level: 6-10. *Earning potential:* 6-10. *Main elements:* hardware, website, services, promotion. *Revenue sources:* ads, subscriptions, sales of services. *Key competences:* web and app development, promotion.

To get access to more information >>> subscribe <<< to our mailing list.

9.Transaction brokers

Difficulty level: 8-10. *Earning potential:* 5-10. *Main elements:* website, processing systems. *Revenue sources:* Transaction fees, monthly subscriptions. *Key competences:* web and app development, promotion.

To get access to more information >>> subscribe <<< to our mailing list.

10. Online businesses without own website.

Difficulty level: 1-4, *Earning potential:* 1-5, *Main elements:* products or creative work, *Revenue sources:* sales/commissions. *Key competences:* skills to make (or outsource) competitive products or skills to make creative work (arts, crafts, designs etc).

To get access to more information >>> subscribe <<< to our mailing list.

Summary:

- There are many different types of online businesses you can start.
- Five basic types of **online revenue sources** are at your disposal:
    1. Sales,
    2. Affiliate Commission,
    3. Subscriptions,
    4. Publishing Ads and
    5. Transaction Fees.
- The **online business models** include but are not limited to:
  – Informative websites, – Online classes and coaching, - Selling digital products,
  – Online Services, – e-Shops, – Interactive websites (Web 2.0), – Market creators,
  – Web Services, – Transaction brokers, – Online businesses without own website
- The simplest online business model **recommended for beginners** is the Informative website

Tasks:

- Make a list of your 3 preferred online business models and revenue sources

In-Depth Readings (Search at Biizly.com):

How to Start an Affiliate Marketing Business from Scratch

10 New Blog Niches to Make Money in 2020 and Beyond

10 Home-Based Earning Opportunities for Moms (and Dads)

Online Business Coaching- Pros & Cons

1.4. Building a Personal Brand and Online Authority

"Your personal brand is a promise to your clients... a promise of quality, consistency, competency, and reliability." - Jason Hartman

At a Glance:

Importance of your personal social profiles for your (future) online business.

Social networks to consider.

What activities to undertake.

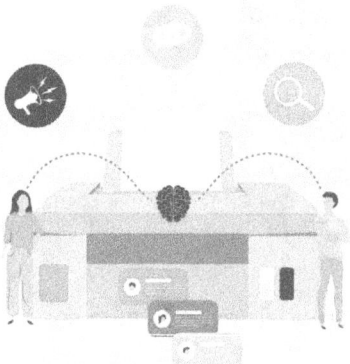

Even before you consider starting a business online, you should **start growing your personal social media profiles**. This is a task you should start doing today. If you don't already have personal profiles on Facebook, Pinterest, Twitter and Linkedin, create them now and get engaged. If you don't want to use your real name use a pen name and stop having excuses.

Your long-term personal presence in the social media is important for several **reasons**:

1. The activity of other people may give you excellent ideas for a business or to refine you own.
2. You can engage with other people that may become your future business partners, customers, consultants or employees.
3. You can establish authority in your field of expertise (or in the field of your future business).
4. You can build a list of loyal followers ready to like/share/buy/advocate your (future) products or services.

5. You could start businesses and fail but your personal profiles will stay with you for a lifetime and they will be there for any business project you start or any now product you offer.

Creating several personal profiles on targeted social media and **not being active is not enough**. You should be engaged in the community by creating quality posts, sharing other peoples' posts, liking, commenting and engaging in meaningful conversations. It is important to **appear relevant, present, knowledgeable and helpful** for the community, especially for your followers (or friends) regarding your expertise or in the field of your planed business. Maybe this is not the only way but is the best way to grow your followers' base, make them loyal and build your online authority on a long run.

Social networks to consider for building your personal brand and authority:

Facebook

Besides most popular, this network is probably the most personal too since it is used to stay in touch with friends and family. The friends and family should be the first and the most eager to share and advocate your (future) business activities and products. That's why a personal presence here is a good idea for everyone who wants to start a business. Besides engaging your friends and family you can also utilize Facebook to build wider audience of followers based on your activity (posting, sharing, commenting) it the area of your expertise or planed future business. The Facebook groups are also excellent place where you can engage in a meaningful way when building your online authority or sharing your business ideas. (Creating a Facebook page for your business is something we will discuss later).

Twitter

Twitter is the most open network of all. Twitter is all about engagement and communication and its mostly done publicly in front of wide audience. Therefore, personal profiles here work better than business profiles. Here you can connect and engage with influencers and potential customers too, so you can learn from them but also build your reputation on a long run. If you focus your activities (tweets, retweets, commenting and following) on specific topic/industry you will eventually build large base of followers ready to consume and advocate your ideas and products.

Linkedin

Linkedin is a network for professionals who are looking to expand their business and/or employment opportunities. If you are considering starting a business that addresses to other businesses (B2B) this network is a must. In some cases, Linedin can help even businesses who deal with the end consumers (B2C) since all professionals are humans first, and have problems, desires and needs. Take for example the stress they have. Anyway, create a profile here if you want to connect with experienced businessman, share and find ideas and get valuable insights in any industry.

Pinterest

More than two-thirds all users on Pinterest are women, especially moms. If you are considering to target woman with your business idea than this network is a must. Most popular topics on Pinterest include: cooking, fashion, nutrition, fitness, weddings and so on. The male target group should also not be forgotten since other popular topics induce: man's fashion, home improvements, home decor, crafts, woodworking, landscaping, gardening etc. While growing your personal presence on Pinterest you can explore new ideas, see what works the best and join some group boards where you can reach your targeted audience very fast after you start your business.

Instagram

Instagram is the second largest social network right after Facebook. It seems that Instagram is reserved for the most popular brands and the so-called influencers. Building a popular profile on Instagram can be challenging since you constantly need appealing photos in order to attract wider audience. Other problem with Instagram, when planning to start a business online, is that you can't attract visitors to your website (with links) unless you pay for advertisement. If you have spare time and capability to constantly create appealing images, try this network too.

Other social networks you could explore before starting your business are YouTube, Reddit, Quora and Tumbler.

Being active in the social media in a fruitful way is a **hard work**. Therefore, you should focus on one, two or **the most on three different social media**. This will depend on your personal preferences, your (future) business type and your target audience. You can also use some tools that will ease and automate your continuous posting on several social media but **being present and personal** is an important aspect when building your personal brand.

Promoting your business (Step 6) is one of the hardest tasks for every new online (or offline) business. Authoritative personal profiles on relevant social media with substantial amount of (loyal) followers can ease spreading the word about your business and products. Such personal profiles can be an excellent starting point for your future business.

Summary:

- Don't wait to start your business first and then to be active on the social media.
- Being active in social media can help you get business ideas, business partners, and employees.
- Focus your posts, shares, commenting, follows and followers in the field of your business idea and/or the fields of your interests and expertise.
- Personal social profiles will help you promote your business (now or in the future).
- Business can come and go. Your personal profiles will stay with you for a lifetime.
- You can use them to promote every business or offer you create in the future.
- Networks to consider Facebook, Twitter, Linkedin, Pinterest, Instagram etc.

Tasks:

- Create personal profiles on Tweeter, Linkedin and/or Pinterest
- Join groups of interest on Facebook and Linkedin
- Join group boards on Pinterest
- Engage (Follow influencers, Post, Share, Comment)

1.5. Some Legal and Other Considerations When Starting a Business Online

At a Glance:

Operating as individual. (No business registration)

Registering a company. (Why and When?)

Copyright issues.

Other considerations: Privacy policy, Security, Disclaimers, Taxation, Legality.

When to incorporate?

One of the best things when starting a business online is that you don't need to register a company right away. Most of the online business models give you the freedom to fully operate your websites and get your earnings as an individual. That is the case in the most countries in the world.

As your revenue grows you may decide to incorporate in order to manage your business more efficiently, like engaging business partners, hire employees, manage the costs of the business, get a merchant account at the bank and so on.

Anyway, some web business models, for example an e-shop, might require that you register a company right away if you want to accept credit and debit cards as payment method since it is the most widely used payment method by the internet users.

Since registering a company requires some finances the best advice here is to postpone the legal registration of your online business until it is necessary from legal and practical reasons. Even in the case of online store, you may decide to accept payments via PayPal only or use some other service that allows individuals to accept banking cards when selling online.

Copyright issues.

Every website needs content, a lot of content. The content may include text articles, images, audios, videos etc. Many internet users assume that everything they can find online can be reused on their sites, but it is not like that. Any resource you find online (and you didn't create it), you cannot simply put it on your website, unless you have permission to do so.

If you don't want to get in some legal trouble when you operate a business stay away from content that you didn't pay for or that is not copyright free. Anyway, there are many free resources online you can still use but some might require giving credit to them (quote the source or the author) if you want to use them on your website.

You also have to be aware that other internet users can steal your original content too. In such cases you should be prepared to protect your legal rights.

Other important issues:
- Privacy policy,
- Disclaimers,
- Online security,
- Taxing,
- Legal, semi-legal and illegal business.
To get access to more information >>> subscribe <<< to our mailing list.

Summary:

- You don't need to register a company right away.
- Reasons to register (early): engage partners and employees, ask for financing, get merchant account.
- Copyright issues:
  - Don't use images (and other materials) if you don't have the rights,
  - Protect your own work.
- Take care of the Privacy policy and Disclaimers.
- Get informed on Online security (yours, your clients' and your website visitors')
- Check the taxation regulations in your country.
- Check the legality of your business idea (globally and locally)

Tasks:
- Make an online research for the issues that concern you the most.

Step 2: Finding the Right Online Business Idea

"New ideas pass through three periods:
1) It can't be done. 2) It probably can be done, but it's not worth doing.
3) I knew it was a good idea all along! "

- Arthur C. Clarke

Key points in Step 2:
- When looking for online business ideas **only the sky is the limit** since the most important factor for success are your determination and persistence.
- There are many **methods and tools** to help you generate business ideas.
- You should search for ideas that fit **your goals, expectations and strengths**.
- When **brainstorming ideas** follow your passion, interests and expertise.
- As a starter, consider ideas that fall into the Differentiating or the Niche Marketing strategy.
- **Differentiation** means being different and/or better than the competitors (in one or more areas of your business).
- **Niche marketing** means serving small market segment unattractive for the other business)
- The selected idea(s) could be **tested for viability and profitability** in order to increase your chances for success.
- When you finally have your business idea, outline a **business concept** to get you going.

Introduction

Every business starts with an idea. Many entrepreneurs have started their business with a single idea, others had many ideas but had to choose only one to pursue. In both cases, business could fail or succeed. As you may know, 7 out of 10 startups fail, but that's the way entrepreneurship works. The **process of generating, filtering and testing business ideas** should decrease the risk of failure but should also give you wider perspective of the available online business opportunities.

The business idea in general could be considered as **a concept for starting and developing a viable business**. Usually it focuses on a **product, service or information** that can solve a problem or satisfy customers' needs. Other important aspects of a business idea are the market size (potential customers) and the revenue mechanism (monetizing potential).

A promising business idea should be *relevant* (must fulfill customers' needs or solve their problems), *innovative*, *unique* and *profitable*. Anyway, it is easier to have many ideas than to turn single one into a successful business. The idea is a good starting point, but its **implementation is also very important**, if not crucial.

The **ideas for an online business** may have some specifics compared to ideas for a traditional business. The online environment provides specific business models and revenue sources. Having that in mind, the online business idea should be related to that specific model. For example, if we want to create an informative website our business idea would simply be a topic that we would cover, like fishing tips, local news, home decorating etc. In other online business models, the idea may come from the way we serve the customers online (online tutoring, live streaming, dating etc.) or from the features a website can provide (communication, blogging service, image editing etc.).

Many **innovations** in the business are not inventing new products or services but delivering the existing in a new way. When it comes to online business ideas, the innovativeness may lay, not in the products or the services themselves, but in the way of presenting them, the methods of pricing, the ways of approaching customers, content richness, website enhancements etc. Amazon didn't invent books but made them available via website and delivered by post. Google didn't invent search engines but made new better search algorithm. E-Bay didn't invent auctions but placed them online.

If you can't find an original idea **duplicate or follow someone else's idea** but do it in a better or a different way. In many cases, having and online business could mean that you copy exactly what other businesses do. If you follow this approach, make sure you choose a trending industry (with a substantial annual growth) or an industry/niche that is not already saturated (too competitive). Even in this approach, doing something better or in a different way will just increase your chances for success on a long run.

Each idea, no matter how brilliant, initially has no real value. A **plausibility check** gives more information about an idea's chances in the marketplace and helps to check its feasibility and profitability. After an idea is finally selected, it enters the implementation phase where it needs conceptualization, resources, management, and in many cases a devoted team.

Tip: If you want to start an online business for the first time, start with an informative website (as business model) and don't waste too much time on finding the right idea. Such online business model requires minimal investment and you can start with more than one project (topic). Experimenting with ideas may bring you a success by circumstance but will surely bring you a valuable experience even if you fail. If it happens that you succeed with the informative web site you can expand your business model, for example by offering online services or opening an e-shop.

2.1. Identifying Acceptable Online Business Ideas

"We all have ability. The difference is how we use it." - Charlotte Whitton

At a Glance:

Identify your goals, expectations, resources and strengths.

Match your idea with a specific business model.

Business strategies: *cost leadership*, *differentiating*, niche marketing.

Before you start your quest for ideas for your online business, you have to make sure you are searching in the right direction. You may encounter a great idea but is it in compliance with your potential, your resources, your goals? Some ideas are simple and don't require much effort and time, other may require specific skills, hard work, many resources, strong team, finances and so on. Having that in mind it is very important to match the idea with your **preferences goals, strengths, resources, and tolerance for risk.**

The online business idea itself is also closely related with a specific online business model, and therefore, before you start looking for ideas you might first select a preferred business model and focus on finding ides suitable for that model. As we believe that the simplest web business model is an **informative website**, you might want to start looking for ideas/topics for your blog or online magazine. Anyway, in your research you may find an idea, (a need) that should be fulfilled with a specific online business model, for example, if there is raising demand for handmade jewelry and you have the skills to make some, you could open an **e-shop** for handmade jewelry. Another example is if you discover that people want ads free email service you should provide such web service charging small monthly or annual fees.

Another important aspect when searching for ideas is that you should be aware of the 3 (three) generic competitive strategies: 1. Cost Leadership, 2 Differentiation and 3, Niche marketing. Not every strategy is appropriate for inexperienced entrepreneurs and new small business.

Being a **price (cost) leader** is the most difficult strategy for small and new businesses. Established business can offer cheaper services and products for several reasons: they have more experience and high productivity, they have large customer base and established partners' network, they can afford low margins and even work with losses if necessary. You might try to be a price leader if you are extra productive (experience craftsmen, fast content writer etc.) or if you live in a low-income country like India or Bangladesh since your living costs would be lower than the average.

Differentiation means that you should try to be different and/or better from your competitors in one or more areas of the business. This may include but is not limited to providing specific features, extra services, high quality, availability, speed of services or something else that will motivate the customers to buy from you and become loyal to your brand. Differentiation may also be accomplished in the communication strategy (channels and way of promotion) or in the barding strategy of your business.

Serving a market niche means that you will try to avoid the (big) competitors by finding a small, unattractive market segment that is not served, or is neglected by the other business. For example, you may want to open a baby store specialized for twins or more narrowly, store for twin baby strollers. The main issue in this strategy is the size of the niche or is it big enough to cover the operating costs of your business. If that's not the case, you may need to find different one or to serve more than one niche.

The Differentiation and the Niche Marketing strategy (or their combination) could work fine for new and small business. So, when looking for ideas you should ask yourself if you could be different and/or better than the competitors that already serve that market or is there an underserved market niche that you can serve profitably.

Summary:

- Make sure your business idea meets your personal preferences, goals, competences and available resources.
- Decide if you prefer specific online business model and search ideas that fit in.
- When searching for Ideas, make sure they can give you freedom to be different from the competitors and/or to be better (at least in some aspects of the business).
- To avoid competition (that is vigorous) work on ideas that address under-served profitable market niches.

Task:

- Name at least one business idea for your 3 preferred business models and revenue sources. (Task done in Step 1 part 3.)

In-depth readings (Search at Biizly.com):

Assessment: Identify Your Entrepreneurial Personality Type

9 ways to know if you have a great business idea

Porter's Model of Generic Strategies for Competitive Advantage

2.2. Generating Online Business Ideas

"The best way to have a good idea is to have lots of ideas." – Linus Pauling

At a Glance:

Brainstorming ideas

Template for writing and grading ideas

Common and online methods for generating ideas

Filtering and selecting the best idea(s)

One of the first obstacles for the newbie entrepreneurs, when starting an online business, is to find the right idea that is worthy to peruse.

Some have no clue where to start, others may be convinced that they already have the wining idea, and some may have many ideas but aren't sure if they have any value. In any case, enhancing your initial list of ideas is always a good idea. At the end, you will have to narrow your choices, but you have to be sure that you are not missing or neglecting the most promising ideas that suite your expectations and capabilities.

There are several methods and tools that will help you generate new ideas for your online business or enhance your existing list. The methods listed below could be combined in order to get the best results in this phase.

(If you believe that you already have the best possible idea for your online business skip to 2.3 Testing Your Online Business Idea(s).)

BRAIN STORMING

Brain storming is a simple technique where you write down all ideas that come into your head no meter how silly or brilliant, they seem at first glance. You may do this method by yourself or you can get help from friends and family. Use our template at biizly.com/ideas-list .

You may start the list with: business you always wanted to do, website and services you already use, business your friends use, popular or new products and services, websites you regularly visit or encountered sometimes, how would you do something better, problems that need to be solved, wishes and needs for specific products or services etc.

Use the other methods below to enhance your list with more ideas that are not just circumstantial but have some logic, reasoning behind them.

In addition to your different ideas you may want to grade (low, average, high) the ideas according to your preference, the earning potential and level of competition. The ideas that you are not willing to pursue just shouldn't be put on the list. Regarding the earning potential and the competition level, just do rough guesses in order to estimate the general attractiveness of each idea. (The true earning potential of the ideas depends on many factors as market size, competition, substitutes, needed resources, your capacity, costs, margins etc., what is something we might try to research later.)

The ideas with bad scores in all areas (low earning potential, low preferences, high competition) should be eliminated right away. The ideas that you have high preference for but have low earning potential are probably bad ideas too; anyway, don't overrule them till you test their profitability. The ideas with high earning potential seem to be the most attractive but they may be also attractive for the competitors too. The competition level is very important aspect when we search for ideas and we will investigate the real competition after we filter our extensive list of initial ideas.

FOLLOW YOUR PASSION, INTERESTS AND COMPETENCES.

"
"Choose a Job You Love, and You Will Never Have to Work a Day in Your Life"

The best advice you can get when starting a business online (or offline), is to follow your passion and interests. When you love what you do it's not work, is pleasure. The job itself and especially success will motivate you to do more. Only that way you can go a long way and reach your highest potential.

When the internet business environment comes in place, it is very possible that you could turn your passion, skills, knowledge or expertise in a profitable online business. You will be surprised when you discover that people might be ready to pay for your competences no meter how trivial they look at first glance. You can develop e-books, one-on-one trainings, video lessons, you can provide business services and sell them for profits. Anyway, your offering doesn't have to be a service or information, it can also be a product or set of products, like fishing equipment for example, where you can additionally provide reviews and best use cases based on your experience in order to enhance your offering. If it happens that the potential customers are not ready to pay for your product and services, you may provide a free information on your site and earn by publishing ads.

Starting a business based on your competences is the best way to start. Anyway, sometimes it might happen that you hate your field of expertise (education and experience) but the opportunity to create an online business, be your own boss, have flexible hours, can make you fell in love again, this time in the new light of your old expertise. If not, find a new passion and star fresh.

OK, that's easier said than done. Many people struggle to find what motivates them, what they love to do or what they do the best. The following questions may help you find the answer: What do you do most often? What activities you enjoy the most? What do you think you do the best? In what areas you (could) give advice to other people? Do you somehow help anybody? What is your hobby? What do you read in the news? Do you write? Do you do sports or exercise? What is your education? What skills you have gained at work? You may also ask other people what they think you are the best at. Answer to any of these questions may point to your future online business.

The skills and knowledge you can turn in to an online business include but are not limited to (only the sky is the limit): playing an instrument, teaching a language, math, sports, gardening, landscaping, crafts, woodworking, fitness, dieting, dating, traveling, fishing, hiking, acting, singing, drawing, frugal living, saving tips, alternative energy, investing, creating business plans, programming, video editing, knitting, refinancing, parenting etc. Don't look at your skills only as a possibility to start a general business, you can be more specific targeting a niche like "organic food gardening", "handmade embroidery t-shirts", "writing business plans for woman entrepreneurs", "programming courses for career changers" and so on.

The main pitfall when perusing your passion for a business is to get stuck with an idea that doesn't have paying customers or a market big enough to make your venture profitable. To avoid that read further.

SOLVE A PROBLEM, FULFILL A NEED

Very important aspect (or a feature) of every business idea is that it should help people. It should solve a specific problem (quit smoking, fix phone) or should satisfy a need (tasty food, travel abroad, play a game).

If potential customers don't have an urge, don't search for a solution or see no value in the products or services you offer they won't buy (or won't read your information).

In general, all business ideas metaphorically can be compared to candies, vitamins and pain killers. Pain killers are products you must have, and you must have them now. Vitamins are nice to have; they may improve someone's life but not immediately since some conditions take time to improve. Candies are something nobody really needs but people want to have fun, spend time, enjoy life etc. If your idea is a pain killer, great! You just need to reach your market before your competitors do. There is not much convincing there. The pain you customers have will buy the products. On the other hand, if you sell vitamins you will have to find ways (appropriate online marketing methods) to convince your prospects for the benefits of your product and why they should buy from you. The candies are the hardest to sell since there are many competitors and substitutes. Suggestions are that you offer a free version of your product until the consumers get addicted, after what you can offer upgrades, premium features, exclusivity etc. For example, *Candy Crash Saga* and *Clash of the Titans* are free games (among many others) that make millions per day from in-game purchases.

In order to find a need or a problem that needs to be solved start with yourself and your friends and family. In our daily lives, we all come across problems, annoyances or frustrations that we would love to see solved. Here are some examples: products hard to find, information needed yesterday, problematic pet's behavior, needy kids, no local dating options, addictions, anger, tiredness etc. If you want to discover more needs and problems (beyond yours) or to find out if other people have the same problems and therefore search for a solution, you may look into the other idea generating methods below.

After you find an existing problem or a need, you should figure out a way (method) how to fulfill them. Should you offer products in an online store? Should you research and publish information? Should you give advice? Should you write an e-book? Should you blog? Should you build and app? ... and so on. The solution you want to provide should match your competences (skills, experience, expertise) or your willingness and determination to become competent to solve the problem (get training, learn, outsource, recommend someone else's solution etc.).

 Next important questions regarding your idea are;

- if people would be willing to pay for your solution and
- is the market big enough to be profitable?

If people prefer free products or services for your solution (entertainment, general advice etc.) you should consider another monetizing mechanism like publish ads, premium versions or donations. In any case you need a market big enough to be profitable on a long run.

BROWSE THE WEB FOR MORE IDEAS

Besides your own and asking your friends and family for online business ideas you may also browse the web in order to come up with some more great ideas for your future venture.

You may start with some general sources like Twitter where you can use the hashtags #startupideas, #businessidea or at Pinterest Popular. Pinterest is a great social network where people share ideas but many other also make money. Almost any pin (post) you see there, leads to a site what could be someone's online business. There you can find many ideas like travel destinations, diets, workout plans, home decorating ideas, gardening tips, interesting products, fashion clothes etc. The popular page shows you what is popular and that could be a good business idea.

Besides the general sources, there are more specialized web source where you can find suggestions for business ideas or brows someone else's ideas like the Business Ideas page at Entrepreneur.com, the Quora's topic for Startup Ideas (and other related topics) and subredits at Reddit like /r/Startup Ideas, /r/Entrepreneur/ or /r/SomebodyMakeThis/.

For currently poplar and new products you may check at eBay Trending or at Amazon Best Sellers and/or Movers and Shakers where you can go dipper to a specific category.

Finding interesting products at eBay and Amazon that sell good does not necessary imply that you should open an e-store to offer those products yourself but you could consider, for example, starting a review site for those type of products or develop other related content and recommend these products using affiliate links (Examples: "How to decor a wall" – Recommend Wall stickers, "Makeup tutorials" – recommend branded makeup and accessories .) You can also try to develop or create complementary products, let's say unique charms for iPhone.

GOOGLE FEATURES AND TOOLS

Googling is always a great way to discover something new including ideas for an online business. Anyway, here we don't imply to searching from scratch but to some features Google Search has and specific tools provided by Google.

These features and tools provided by Google are probably the best method to generate and refine business ideas, but we put it at the end since you need some sort of initial ideas, topics or industries in mind in order to utilize them. So, you can use these features and tools to refine your ideas, narrow your niche or even discover new, related and existing business opportunities. The great thing of using them is that the suggestions you will get are based on searches done by real people, people that used Google to find products, solve a problem or satisfy a need they have.

The methods described below will also be of great use later for discovering content ideas for your website and for SEO keyword analyses when you optimize your website for the search engines. Google Trends and the Keyword Planer can also be used to test the viability of your business ideas, but we will discuss that in the next section.

Google Related Searches

After you enter the search term when googling, at the bottom of the search results you will get a list of 8 "Searches related to ...". These related searches are the most common searches (besides the one you entered) that users insert into the search engine to describe their informational need. The original purpose of this feature is to help the users find what they are looking for (if they didn't find it in the first 10 results). Anyhow, you can also use this list to refine your idea, find other related ideas or narrow your niche.

For example, if you enter the term "piano tutoring" among the other related searches you will get the term "beginner piano lessons for adults". This may direct you to focus your idea to adult people since you may have experience with them, and you are aware of their specific needs. Another example is that if you enter the term "social phobia", you will discover that people also use the term "social anxiety" to describe the same problem, what you may also want to use to explain your offering, let's say an e-book on overcoming social anxiety.

Be aware that the (search) term itself does not describe your idea completely. That is just a need, for which, you have to find a profitable way (a business model and a product/service) to fulfill.

Google Search Auto Complete

As you start typing at the search bar, Google starts giving you instant suggestions that complete your term (*See image in right*). This feature helps users to enter the term faster or directs them to complete the search they started with the most common searches done by other users. The results that you get with this feature are similar with the related searches described above but with the distinction that it really offers related terms (synonyms), but you can get more suggestions instantly since you can change terms or the first letters as you type. Using the feature, you can find much more ideas to narrow your niche or discover new niches you didn't think of before.

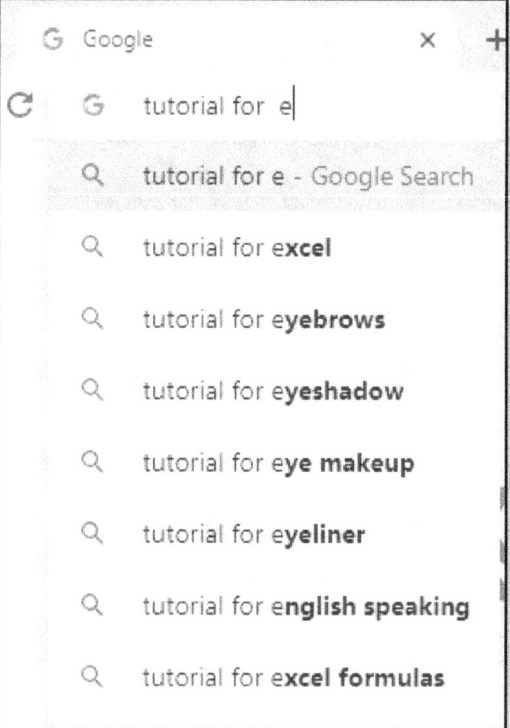

Google Trends

Google Trends is a great tool that can help you generate more ideas, compare ideas head-to-head or initially test your ideas.

The tool shows the popularity of a search term trough time. It doesn't show the absolute number of searches done but uses relative scale from 0 to 100 based on the peak time.

To use Google Trends in your benefit, enter your initial business ideas (or terms used to describe your offering) as search terms. You can also set filters by country or state, time range (we suggest 5 years), category and search type (web, images, YouTube and shopping). As a result, you will get a graph (a trend line) that will show you if the demand for your offering (your potential idea), is rising, is steady or fades away. You can also notice if there is some type of seasonality of your offering, like peak times during summer/winter or during holidays.

By comparing two (or up to five) search terms you could see which term has higher popularity or higher demand. Naturally, the terms with higher popularity could be better business ideas (if we assume that the competition is at the same level).

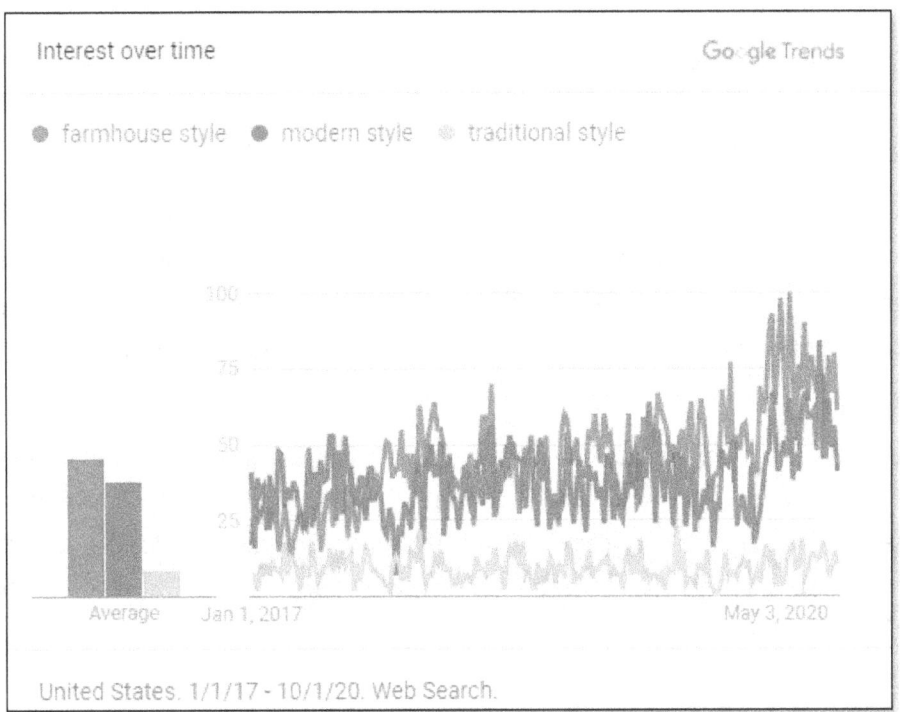

As you can see from the image, it seems that the interest for the "farmhouse style" is rising faster than the interest for the "modern style" while the "traditional style" has steady pace.

The rule of thumb, when entering in a new business, is that you go for ideas that have rising demand and stay away of ideas that have declining trend, however, that's not always the best advice. For example, the tool may help you find rising niche in a fading industry like "healthy dessert" vs "deserts".

Using Google trends to test ideas will be discussed later, but at this point you can use it to get a good perspective if some business is viable or not. You can simply use it to eliminate some ideas, especially when you compare them with other ideas and topics in the same or similar industry. The tool will also give you up to 25 related queries and topics that you can use to discover new business opportunities.

Note: Do not use this tool to eliminate ideas by comparing mainstream ideas to niche market ideas (earrings vs. handmade earrings). Obviously, the mainstream idea will have much higher popularity but will also have much higher competition, something we can't check with this tool.

Google Keyword Planner

The Keyword Planner Tool is part of Google Ads, the online advertising service. In order to use this tool, you have to create an account, there but you won't pay any fees until you start advertising.

The distinctive features of this Google tool, compared to the others described above, are that it gives a huge number of related keywords (search terms), it gives the approximate volume of monthly searches, the level of competition (low, medium, high) based on number of advertisers, the range of bid in $ to get top position of the ad.

The huge list of related keywords may give you additional ideas for more niches or it could help you to narrow your niche. The volume of monthly searches will give you a general idea of the demand for your offering. The price range for a bid to get a top position in the ads gives you an idea how profitable your niche is, but it also is an indication for the level of competition. Higher bids mean higher competition.

The high bids are usually a great indicator for profitable business ideas, for example if you want to start an informative web site in a specific industry and run Google ads where you can make high earnings per click. Anyway, the question here is if you could bring any visitors to your site since the competition is enormous, especially for these industries.

As you can see, with the use of Google Trends and the Keyword planner for generating online business ideas you actually start the testing of your business ideas too, what is something we want to do next.

FILTERING YOUR IDEAS

At the end of your quest for generating online business ideas you should get a list of reasonable ideas that you are interested and willing to implement. Your list may reach as many as 100 ideas but you should start filtering them using your common sense or some of the above mentioned indicators (preference, rising trends, high volume, high bids, variety of niches you could cover in an industry/topic and so on).

Before you begin to test your ideas, you should narrow you list to no more than 10 ideas (5 would be ideal) since testing each idea could take much time and resources. Anyway, you may start testing your ideas one by one, and choose the first idea that meets your expectations and goals. If none of the pre-selected ideas passes the feasibility test (the next part) you can always go back to your longer list and test some more ideas.

Summary:

- Start brainstorming online business ideas (and write them down) using the described methods.
- Even if you already have some ideas, enhance your list with more.
- Use the described tools to pre-test your ideas and to discover more business opportunities.
- Filter and prioritize your enhanced list of ideas using some criteria as personal preference, your competences, rising trends, expected profitability, competition etc.
- Choose your 5 best ideas (or less) and take them in to the testing phase.

Tasks:

- Make a list of ideas (Use our template at biizly.com/ideas-list)
- Grade the ideas using common sense
- Select and rank your 5 best ideas

In-depth readings (Search at Biizly.com):

Profitable Online Business Ideas (Examples)

This is how I came up with 100 business ideas

9 Unusual Business Ideas We Love

Frighteningly ambitious start up ideas.

Five start-ups that are tackling life's annoying problems

29 Creative Thinking Exercises on How to be Creative

2.3. Testing Your Online Business Idea(s)

"

"Everything starts with the customer." – June Martin

At a Glance:

Should you put your online business idea(s) on test and why?

Google tools for testing business ideas.

Is your idea profitable? Can you fight the competition?

Surveying the potential customers.

Validating online business ideas with landing pages.

The crowdfunding test.

Before investing in a new business, you need to test your idea's true potential. You surely don't want to put your stakes into an idea only to discover later that no one likes to buy your product or use your service. Therefore, you should do your best to check if there's a paying market for your offering, is the market big enough, what is the level of the competition and if your idea is profitable on long run.

Whether you have been creative and generated tons of great ideas, you pre-selected 5 promising ideas (like we have suggested) or you have a single "winning" idea, you should first make sure if they are viable and worthy to peruse.

Big investments might need comprehensive market research done by professionals, but that requires substantial finances and time. Fortunately, online entrepreneurs and small business owners have at disposal many free (or affordable) methods for testing online business ideas. If you don't feel comfortable with any of the methods described below, or you don't have the time, you could always hire an affordable and experienced freelancer to do the testing for you.

Regardless of what you decide to do, you should be aware that there is no definite way to tell if an idea would be successful or not. The final verdict will be given by the market itself when your business is up and running. Anyway, any type of research can reduce the risks and can help you make more informed decisions. Therefore, we suggest that you at least use the Google's Keyword Planer (described below) to test your idea.

In the cases where testing the idea costs more (time, resources and nerves) than starting the business itself (like an informative website model) you could skip this phase and go to 2.4. Outline a Business Concept, before you establish your online presence in Step 3.

Tip: Instead of doing your own research try to find if some did it already. Google "<<your idea>> industry report" or ""<<your idea>> market analysis" and you may be surprised that many useful information might be available freely on the web. For more updated information, filter the search to only include results from the past year.

GOOGLE TOOLS FOR TESTING BUSINESS IDEAS

When we talked about generating online business ideas, we also discussed Google Trends and Google Keyword Planner. They are great for initial testing of the validity of your business ideas too. Since these tools are based on real searches done by real people, they are great indicator for the validity of almost any business idea. They only lack a clear picture about the competition (their presence and strength), but that is something you need to analyze further, after you initially test your idea with these tools.

Google Trends

The purpose behind Google Trends for testing business ideas is to discover if your industry or niche has a rising trend or not.

The best businesses to enter are the ones that have rising trends, and that's for several reasons. As new customers enter the market, they may not be aware of the existing products and brands so you can earn their attention and their money more easily than in established and saturated industries. Another reason is that the existing businesses might not be prepared to satisfy the rising demand. On the other hand, the worst industries to get in are those that have declining trends. Make sure you avoid declining industries and at least choose ideas that have steady demand in the recent years.

After you enter search term in Google Trends that describes your business idea or offering (industry, niche, product, feature, need, problem or similar), you will get a trend line (select 5 or 3 years). The trend line does not show the actual volume of searches but a relative one based on peak times. If you want to get clearer picture about the volume of searches done, check the same search term in the Google Keyword Planner. When using Google trends, you can narrow your search by setting filters by country or state, time range, category and the search type (web, images, YouTube and shopping). Monitor the graph for any long term or seasonal trends and also observe the suggestions to discover some related terms that may have rising trends.

Besides observing the trends, the tool is also great to compare different ideas especially if they are in the same industry. Comparing ideas from different industries might be tricky since they most probably have different profitability and different level of competition. Anyway, you may just compare the trends to choose the one that has a rising one.

There is no doubt that Google trends is useful tool, but be aware of several downsides you may encounter:

- a single search term not always represents your business idea as a whole (you may need to test several search terms to get a better picture for the entire industry or niche)
- there might be some rising niches in declining industry (and vice versa)
- users may have changed/altered the search terms for same issue over time
- when testing a niche, always use quotations to monitor the actual searches for that term and exclude related terms.

Google Keyword Planner

While Google Trends gives you the trend of a search term (rising, steady, falling), the Keyword planer gives you the volume of searches (in ranges 0-10,10-100,100-1000 etc.) and also the level of competition. The level of competition (high, medium, low) is not based on all competitors but only those who advertise for that search term using Google Ads. The price range for bids to get a top position in Google indicate the level of competition, but the profitability of that niche/term too.

The volume of monthly searches will give you a general idea of the demand for your offering. The higher the volume, the better. Anyway, we should be more interested in the profitability of a given search term per, let's say, 100 visitors. The profitability of search term may vary per business, since not every business has same costs and same efficiency.

Great indicator for the profitability of the search terms (and the industry) could be the bid height, what this tool also presents. If a company pays a $1 per click (bid height) for an ad they would expect at least $100 profits (not counting the ad costs) per 100 visitors or they will make loses. If we multiply the monthly volume with the bid height, we can get the overall profitability of a search term what we can use to compare the profitability of different ideas (niches, industries etc.). (For the profitability of an industry, you should also analyze the competition.)

Unfortunately, the tool cannot tell us if we can reach the customers more efficiently than our competition and be more cost-efficient in order to achieve the same or higher profitability. Having this in mind, if we want to estimate the true profitability potential of our ideas, we should also analyze the strengths and weaknesses of the competitors in the light of our ambitions and capabilities.

REVIEWING THE COMPETITION

One of the best ways to test your ideas, or even to get new, is to analyze the competition in your selected industry or niche. Actually, reviewing the competition is something you shouldn't miss when starting a new business and you should at least do a quick glance in the industry you get in.

There are many reasons why you would like to review your competition. When you analyze the competitors, you can discover their way of doing business, the products and services they offer, the quality of their site and content, their straights and weaknesses and so on. The process may help you understand the landscape better, refine your idea, narrow your niche and learn how to position your business for success – capitalizing on the competitors' weaknesses and your own straights.

Since, in this phase of your business journey you want to test your idea's feasibility, besides on the profitability, you should focus on the quantity and the quality (of the main) competitors and your ability to get into that picture.

The presence or absence of competition can give you insightful information about the plausibility and profitability of your idea. Don't just assume that your idea is unique and there are no competitors. Unless you discover a cure for cancer, teleportation device or another extraordinary invention, you will most certainly encounter competition, even if it's an indirect one. Anyway, if somehow happens that your idea has no competitors (or just few), you eider found you self a gold mine, or (most probably) your idea is worthless, since there are not enough paying customers for it.

If there are no, or there are just few competitors for your business idea, be careful. Before you start you venture, first ask/test you potential customers if they would be willing to pay for your products or services, for what reasons and under what conditions. If you manage to get enough favorable answers about your idea, you are on the right track.

A large number of competitors tells us a different story. On one side, many competitors signal a profitable industry since everybody wants to go where the money is. On the other side, you have to know that it's not easy to run a business in a competitive industry ... unless you are getting into a trending one (with fast annual growth rates) or you have something superior to offer.

While the number of the competitors signals the profitability of an industry (or a niche), their quality (strengths) will actually show if there is a real business opportunity for you. If you can spot weaknesses in the majority of the competitors where you can fill in – there is your chance, but if the competition seems so strong and flawless and you have nothing new or different to offer you should probably modify your idea (pick a niche market) or go step back and test a new, different idea.

So, since in the most cases you will encounter competition, the question is how you can get a piece of the pie. To do so, you will have to try to be better different (in some or all aspects of the business), or you should find an underserved profitable niche(s). (We previously discussed strategies how you can fight (or avoid) the competition with differentiation and niche marketing).

If the landscape is not that competitive, or the competitors didn't fully exploit all online marketing channels, you could try to enter the market by mimicking successful online business. Anyway, on a long run, you will have to differentiate your business and develop recognizable brand in your industry (or niche) in order to protect and grow your market share.

Hint: If you want to start an online business for a first time and you don't plan to invest much money into it at the beginning, don't waste too much time for reviewing the competition since almost all profitable industries will have many competitors. The good news is that they are not perfect so you can learn how to compete with them over time.

Where to find the competitors?

The most straightforward way to discover your competitors is to Google your industry or your niche using search terms that describe your business or your offering.

Note: In many cases, as you search, instead of competitors' sites you may get well known sites (Wikipedia, YouTube, reddit, Quora, Pinterest) , sites that combine offerings (or links) of more than one competitor (eBay, Amazon, Etsy, local directories) or articles related to the search term (best xyz, how to xyz, what is xyz). Such results may widen the perspectives for your business giving you clues where you may want to place or promote your offering (besides on your own website). Anyway, if you get such search results but you still want to discover your direct competitors you should refine your search terms adding niches, location, features or words like store, company, provider etc., depending on your business type and industry.

When using Google to discover competition, the first 10 results in the list (first page) could be considered as your most vigorous competitors and you should (at least) analyze these. If the list continues to the second (and third) page you should probably consider narrowing your niche or abandoning your idea completely unless... you could offer something better or slightly different that will attract customers to you instead to your competitors.

Other sources you may consider when searching for your competitors, depending on your business idea, are: Amazon, eBay, Facebook, Twitter, Pinterest, LinkedIn, Yelp, Craigslist, Yellow Pages and so on. Besides the abovementioned, there are probably many other places (sources) where you can find your competitors online.

What to analyze?

After you discover your direct competitors, you should make a list and start analyzing their way of doing business and their strengths and weaknesses. Analyze at least 3 to 5 competitors but there is no need to go over 10 since it might take a lots of time. (If you have selected narrow niche with no competitors analyze the competition in the closest offering to yours).

While a big number of competitors (in general) indicates a profitable idea, you should also check if you could beat or at least match the prices of their offerings. If you are not able to match the prices, you should consider offering extra value to your customers by offering premium services, freebies, extra features, extraordinary customer service etc. To check the profitability of your idea you should also check if your competitors advertise and how much they spend. Besides Google Keyword Planner you can try services like SEMrush, Spyfu, and Ispionage where you can "spy" your competitors if, and how much they advertise. If they advertise on a long run, it is almost certain sing that the idea is profitable.

The analyzes of the strengths of the competition should teach you how to improve your business and your offering, the weaknesses on the other hands could show if you could fill in, or where you could capitalize the most. Actually, your entire business idea might be based on the major weaknesses of the existing competition in certain industry.

To analyze your competition and discover their strengths and weaknesses you should review some or all of the following aspects:

- time in business (use Wayback Machine https://archive.org/web/)
- website usability and structure (speed, navigation, user experience etc.)
- home page, about page, portfolio, contact page etc.
- website traffic and traffic sources (use tools like alexa.com, SEMrush, ahrefs)
- call to action (email subscriptions, give always, promotions)
- products (landing pages, pictures, features, quality, prices, discounts, etc.)

- customer service (delivery, returns, warranties etc.)
- blog (topics, frequency of posting, comments, etc.)
- content quality (text, images, videos)
- keywords they use (titles and subtitles, bolding, in text, in links etc.)
- level of SEO (positions at google, inbound links, SEO tools in use etc.)
- social media (buttons positions on the site, number of followers/likes, number of likes and shares on posts, frequency of posting, engagement in discussions etc.)

The competitor's site and social media pages are great sources to analyze but you can get even more insights by subscribing to their mailing list too and analyze the content and their strategy there.

Since Google is a major traffic source for most of the websites, you should analyze their level of SEO (Search engine optimization) but you should also check their social media pages to get the complete picture. The most important social media sites include Facebook, Twitter, Pinterest and Instagram. You should do this not only to discover their online marketing tactics but also to discover if they efficiently exploit all online marketing channels available. For example, if your competitors are not present or aren't active on Pinterest that might be a great business opportunity for you.

If you spot any weaknesses in the areas mentioned above or if there are possibilities to offer something better or different, something that will attract customers to your offering, there might be your business opportunity. On the other hand, if the completion is strong, has no major weaknesses and you have no ideas how to be better or different you should probably consider different idea.

Let's conclude. When you test your online business idea, you should analyze the competition for two major reasons. The first one is to find out if your idea is profitable, the second one is to see if you are capable to compete in that industry (or a niche) and get a piece of that pie. You also may want to refine and improve your idea based on the competitors' strengths and weaknesses. The observation and analyzes of the competition should continue even after the start of your business in order to further improve your business and defend your positions.

SURVEYING THE POTENTIAL CUSTOMERS

Previously (the above methods for testing ideas) you investigated the need (demand) for your offering using some Google tools, you observed the performance of your competitors and you found areas and gaps where you and your business idea may fit. Anyway, none of these can predict the real success of your future business. Therefore, the best way to put your business idea on test is (directly) to ask/survey or test your potential customers (or audience). It really doesn't matter if you think your idea is cool and promising one, it only matters that you can reach (real) consumers that see value in your offering, really want it and are willing to pay for it.

There are several approaches you can use in order to get the desired response from your target audience. You may ask direct questions, you may try to validate your idea with a landing page (subscriptions, pre-orders, MVP) or you can make a crowd-funding test. Some of these approaches are free, they will just consume your time, but other may require some finances to get the best results. You don't need to use all methods but only the one which you think is the most appropriate.

Target Audience

Regardless of what method(s) you choose to approach your customers, first you need to define your target market and the places where you can find and approach them. You may assume that everyone is your potential customer but identifying your perfect (best profile) customers will bring you better success not only in the survey but also later in the business.

When defining your target audience, first think about basic demographics like gender, age, location, family income, and education levels. Include information that is relevant to your product offerings, such as hobbies, interests, and life goals. Next, consider if your potential clients will use search engines and what search terms would they use to find you or would they encounter your offering at other sites. Finally, determine where (online and offline) you can find and approach your target market in order to test your business idea.

Since it is so simple, you may decide first to survey your friends (offline and on social media) and may also ask them to share your posts (spread the word) to their friends too. The question here is if this way you could get honest and enough answers.

Besides your personal profiles at the social media as starting point, other sites where you can reach your target audience for free and more precisely include Reddit, Quora, Craigslist and many forums on different topics. Any of these sites have certain rules that you have to follow if you want to have chance to ask your questions or get hits on your testing/questioning pages. For example, at Reddit you need to have aged profile and positive Karma (score) in order to post in some subreddits (topics).

If you have difficulties, reaching your target audience via the free sources you should consider placing ads at Google Search, Facebook or other sites that gather your target audience. For a small budget, you can test your business idea targeting your audience by search terms they use (Google search) or by precise demographics and interest (Facebook). For this purpose, you can even use the free ad coupons offered to first time customers at these advertising platforms.

Another handy online service that can help you create the surveys and reach your target audience is Google Surveys, where at affordable rates you can research the viability of your business idea.

For some business ideas, you may want to survey your customers offline, for example, at Starbucks or at the local mall if the visitors there meet your definition of your target audience and you have the skills and will to do the questioning.

When your idea targets other business as your customers (B2B), you may approach them onsite or via phone or email. If that's the case for your business idea you will easily find at least a sample of 20 to 30 potential clients using Google, Yelp, Foursquare, Yellow pages or other business directories.

Interviews and questionnaires

After you define your target customers and the sites where you can approach them it is time to ask some questions. This activity can be done through interviews and/or questionnaires.

The interviews are done in person (in real time) regardless if it is onsite, by phone or by e-messengers. This method is more time consuming, but you can ask more complex questions and sub-questions and get answers that are more detailed.

The questionnaire is a form that consists of series of questions and it is distributed (offline or online) to the respondents. This method is more suitable to get more answers in shorter amount of time. You can easily prepare a questionnaire in Google forms, distribute the link to the target audience and get automated analytics too.

The questions you may ask your potential customers can include but are not limited to:

- Do you have a need for such and such product (or service)?
- Do you already use similar product and from which providers?
- How much you spend for such products monthly/yearly?
- What you like and dislike in the products you already use?
- What new or improved features would you like to see in the product?
- How much would you be ready to pay for an improved product?
- Would you switch from your current supplier and why (why not)?
- Would you like to make a pre-order from us?
- Would you like to try/buy our new product when is ready, and under what conditions?
- Are you willing to give use your e-mail address in order to inform you when the product is available at the market?

If you don't have precise targeting it is good idea to ask for the respondents' characteristics like age, gender, location, income, education, interest etc.

Also, make sure your list of questions is not too long. Make it answerable in no longer than 15 minutes and point that out on the start of the questioning.

After you design the questions, you should distribute them to your target audience through the selected channels. It is very important that you get at least 30 (honest) answers at minimum, let's say 10% response rate (30 answers form 300 questioned). If you cannot achieve that, there are at least tree possibilities. The first possibility could be that the market is too small, next is that your offering is not attractive enough and the third is that you are having trouble reaching your target audience. In each case, this is not a good sign for your idea since you may encounter any of these after you start your business.

After you collect enough answers you should analyze them. Not all answers should be favorable in order to recognize a good business idea. The rate of favorable answers that will indicate a promising business would vary depending on the market size, numbers of competitors, product familiarity, etc. For example, if the market is big enough to fit 10 profitable competitors and you get 20% favorable answers (6 out of 30) you are on a great track. If you get less than 3 favorable answers entering that business could be riskier.

The answers of all respondents, favorable or not, may also help you sense the attractiveness for your future product, the real need of the customers, and the weaknesses (and strengths) of the competition. All this can give you hints to improve your business ideas and business model and test your offering one more time if necessary.

If the potential clients are not aware for the need of your product or are reluctant to change current suppliers but you still believe that your offering will bring more value to them, you should make sure that there is a way you can convince them to try and change supplier before you start your business, not after. In some cases, offering free samples or trial version could do the work, but sometimes you will have to put much effort and resources. Otherwise, start looking for another online business idea.

VALIDATING ONLINE BUSINESS IDEAS WITH LANDING PAGES

Approaching your customers and asking them questions regarding your business idea is a great way to apprise the potential market and the attractiveness of your product in the light of the present competition. Anyway, questioning your potential customers may be tricky. It might happen that you best customers are too busy or reluctant to answer questions. The respondents may also give untruthful answers because they are in hurry, they are being polite, or they didn't understand the question. At the end, when your real offering is ready and presented to them, they might act differently from the answers they gave.

Having this in mind, it comes out that the best way to test the target market is to create real market environment and check if the potential clients are ready to give us something of value (e-mail address or money) for our (still in development) products or services.

Testing online business ideas with lending pages comes in several different scenarios:

- **Subscriptions** (Present the idea and ask the potential customers their e-mail address in order to stay in touch and inform them for the future activities.)
- **Pre-order** (Ask the visitors to register in order to get the featured product first.)

- **Pre-sales** (Ask the visitors to pay some amount in advance in order to get the product when is ready.)
- **Selling MVP** (Make a product with minimal acceptable features (minimal viable product) and if customers buy – develop the full version)
- **Mimic sales page** (Act as if the product is ready and fully functional and test if the customers are ready to spend money on it by hitting the order button)

If you decide to use any of these methods for testing your market, you will need a landing page (at least free subdomain and hosting). Despite the free resources to do this, we would suggest that you establish your real web presence (Step 3) so you can make your landing pages feel and look more legitimate and more reliable to the potential customers.

After you create the landing pages, next task in this method would be to bring visitors to your pages and observe the reaction of your potential customers. Since bringing visitors to your site is not that easy you should consider paying for ads and precisely target you preferred audience. You can use Google Ads and Facebook Ads and try to get free coupons as first-time customer.

THE CROWDFUNDING TEST

Crowdfunding is a method of funding a venture or a project by raising small amounts of money from a large number of people online. Crowdfunding is great for rising money but is also a great way to validate your business idea. Namely, rewards-based crowdfunding platforms like Indiegogo and Kickstarter enable start-ups to get finances from the individual investors in exchange for gifts or future products.

If enough people like your business idea and are willing to finance your business in return for your future products is certainly a great sign for your business. The finances you will acquire and the pre-sales you make will ensure a smooth start of your business.

Crowdfunding platforms can bring many people to see your business idea, but do they match your target market, do they understand your offering, or do they need your product type at all? Therefore, if your idea fails the crowdfunding test but you still believe in its potential, you should try using other validating methods. Anyway, potential investors may give you useful information about your business idea and products, and how to make them better.

***

After you test the validity of your business ideas using (some of) the above-mentioned tools and methods you should **make your final decision** which idea you are going to pursue. Criteria for choosing your best idea could include: your personal preference (intuition, confidence, competences, skills), earning potential (industry/niche profitability), market size (monthly searches/number of customers), competition strength.

Summary:

- There are several methods to test the validity of your business idea
- Google Trends will show you if your idea is in trending (rising), steady or falling industry. Always prefer the first.
- Google Keyword Planer will show you the attractiveness of your idea based on actual monthly searches done by real users. By using this tool you can also sense the profitability of your idea.
- Reviewing the competition will indicate the profitability of your idea, the level of competitiveness (is it hard or easy to do business there) and your ability to fit in.
- Surveying the potential customers can give you a realistic prediction for the success of your business idea.
- The final verdict of your business idea will be given by the market itself after you lunch your product, but testing the idea with landing pages or the crowdfunding test can bring your idea closest to real market conditions where you can test before you fully devote to it..
- At the end of the process of testing your business idea(s) you should decide which idea (if any) is worthy to be executed.

Tasks:

- Start testing your idea(s) one by one. (Use at least the Google Keyword Planer)
- Finally decide which single idea to implement.

In-Depth Readings (Search at Biizly.com):

Simple Ways to do Market Research Online

Tools to Analyze Your PPC Competition

Sites to get Unbiased Feedback on Your Business Idea

Setup a landing page for testing a business or product idea.

Crowdfunding to test the Minimum Viable Product (MVP)

2.4. Outline a Business Concept for Your Online Business Idea

> " *"Ideas are worth nothing unless executed."* - Steve Jobs

At a Glance:

What is the first step for bringing your idea to reality?

Writing a full Business Plan requires skills and time.

One-page Business Concept is simpler and faster approach.

Business Concept Form Template to Download.

Whether you have used common sense, trusted your instincts, or have tested your idea's viability, **at this point, you should have selected a single promising idea** that best fits your goals and expectations. Besides that, you should also be willing and eager to take your idea into the implementation phase. Having the right online business idea is just the beginning of your long to go online business journey.

Developing a business concept should be the first step towards the execution of your business idea. Having a business concept in your mind only, is not such a bad thing, but putting it in writing will give you better perspective and a solid strategic guide to follow into the implementation process. We can view the business concept as a bridge between an idea and a **business plan**. Since writing a business plan is not an easy task, and could take long time, you could leave it for the later stages of your business (if necessary). On the other hand, the business concept is representing the same reasoning, but is much simpler and will take less time and less effort to create. Anyway, if you want to attract investors or get a loan from a bank, you will certainly need a well-written business plan, and in such case, the written business concept will help you prepare the business plan too.

A Business Concept for your online venture should be no longer than one page and could include the following elements:

- Name of your business (prospective one)
- Domain name (registered or desired variations)
- Unique selling proposition (A slogan on what distinguishes you from the competitors)
- Mission statement (Reason of existence, target market, problem you solve or need you satisfy and how.)
- Brief description of your products and services
- Online business model and revenue source(s)
- Web content strategy (Product and services only, Blog posts, Video content, Customer generated content, etc.)
- Internet marketing strategy (Where and how you will rich your target market.)

In order to write down your business concept use our form (biizly.com/bc) or simply use the Online Business Checklist (biizly.com/cl) where you can also mark your progress (The Business Concept is also embedded in the Checklist).

If you are not able or you are unwilling to fill out everything in the form right away, read some examples or leave it for later, but continue to read and to implement the instructions in the Guide. (As a real online entrepreneur, you shouldn't allow small obstacle to stop you at your journey.)

Now that you have outlined the business concept, completed or not, written or in your mind, you are ready to make your biggest step, to actually start your online business.

Summary:

- Your business idea has no value unless implemented.
- As a first step towards execution of your idea, you should at least outline a Business Concept.
- A business concept in your mind only is not a bad idea but having a written one is a better option.
- The Business concept shouldn't be longer than a page, should help you clarify your business idea and could serve as a strategic guide for starting and running your online business.
- Developing a comprehensive business plan is not an easy task and if it is not necessary at this stage of your business, you can rely only on your business concept.

Task:

- Outline the business concept of your business idea
  (Download the form at biizly.com/bc)

In-depth readings (Search at Biizly.com):
How to Write a Business Concept Paper
Examples of a Business Concept
Examples of Unique Selling Propositions
Techniques for Crafting a Mission Statement

Step 3: Establishing Web Presence for Your Online Business

"

"Websites promote you 24/7: No employee will do that." — *Paul Cookson*

Key points in Step 3:
- To establish your web presence you need a domain name, hosting and a website builder/system.
- Finding the right domain name ($15/year) is not an easy quest since all the good names are already taken.
- Eventually, you will pinpoint a decent domain name using your creativity (or help).
- As website management system, our suggestion is to use WordPress (besides some other options) since it is easy to use, free, reliable, flexible, most widely used and can meet all your needs for a website.
- Acquiring a reliable hosting for your website won't cost you much (>$5/month) but is one of the key investments in you online business.
- Start your initial website fast (initial settings, some content and social media profiles), afterwards build your online business gradually (Steps 4, 5 and 6).

Step 3: Establishing Web Presence for Your Online Business

Introduction

Now that you have selected your best online business idea and you have outlined the business concept; it is time to dive into the (not so) deep waters of the web business environment. The first two steps of the guide were meant to prepare you for the definite start of you online venture in this step. Here in Step 3 you will actually begin to see the first outcomes of your effort. You may go a long way until you fully implement your business concept online but establishing your **initial web presence** is the first tangible step toward that goal and you should do it **as soon as possible**.

Besides creating a website for your online business venture, you may need to establish **web presence for your traditional (offline) business** too. Having a website is a must for every business nowadays since the modern consumers heavily rely on search engines and maps to find products, services, information and locations.

To establish web presence, or to start the website for your business, you will fist need to **register a domain name** and get/install a website management system (**website builder**) together with a **hosting plan**. This is actually much simpler than it may sound for a rooky. You (yes you in particular) could put your initial website up and running for 30 minutes or less*.

To complete your initial web presence, after providing the above mentioned essentials (domain + hosting + web system), you will need to make some basic adjustments on the site, add some initial content like simple homepage, description, about page, contact information etc., and to set your social media profiles.

There are several reasons why you would like to start your initial web site fast. First of all, it will give you the filling of creating something of value and you will prove yourself that starting a business online is a no-brainer. All of that will highly motivate you to go further and carry out the steps that follow. The other reasons for going online as soon as possible are described later.

Having an online business doesn't always imply that you must have your own website and a domain. You can simply sell products on eBay or Amazon. You can sell your handicrafts at Etsy, or you can sell your arts and designs on sites such Fine Art America, CafePress or Zazzle. You can also offer your services on freelancing sites like Fiverr, Freelancer or Upwork, you could become a Youtuber or you can place your e-books or apps on App Store or Play Store. Anyhow, regardless of these online earning opportunities, it is always a good idea to start building your own e-brand with an appealing domain name and a nice website.

3.1. Naming Your Online Business and Registering a Domain Name

*"Domains have and will continue to go up in value
faster than any other commodity ever known to man." – Bill Gates*

At a Glance:

Should you register a company or get the domain first?

Good domain names are hard to find but there are still some opportunities.

Approaches to find the perfect domain name.

One of the best things when starting an online business is **that you don't need to register a company (right away)** in order to start your operations. You can fully operate your online business as an individual and earn for living, or even make millions. Since registration of a company may involve additional costs, many online entrepreneurs decide to skip or postpone the registration of a legal entity and operate as individuals.

Having the advantages in mind, we recommend that you go **as an individual** first, and **register a domain name only (biizly.com/hostgator01).***** The registration of the domain will mark the official start of your online business. The domain can then be used/perceived as a name for your online business too. If you decide to incorporate later, you

---

***** From time to may recommend the best available (and affordable) services for your business. For recommending some of these services may receive affiliate commission, but you won't pay a higher price for the products.

can transfer the ownership of the domain name, if necessary, to the newly registered company.

Regardless of the approach you choose, naming your legal business and registering a domain name are two separate procedures. Anyhow, if you want to match your business name with your domain name, you should select/register the domain name first, since it is fairly hard to find a desirable domain name that is available. Afterwards, you can name your legal business accordingly, incorporating the legal requirements for a business name in your country. For example: As the domain is Biizly.com the name of the company could be "Biizly.com Online Investments Ltd." or "Biizly Web Consulting Gmbh." or "Biizly Publishing Inc".

It is not uncommon that a company owns more than one domain. In such case the domains may represent, not the company itself but different projects or different brands owned by that company. The same thing applies for individuals too. You may own as many domains as you wish and can have more than one online project or brand.

SEARCHING FOR THE PERFECT DOMAIN NAME.

"I often get questioned about how we came up with the name Weebly. We all know that all of the good domain names are already taken, and we had neither the desire nor budget to try and fit our business into a pre-existing word – so we made one up." – David Rusenko

Since the domain name is very important for your online business, the effort you will put to find an appealing one is completely worth it. Anyway, let's get straight right ahead. Finding a good domain name for your online business is damn hard. You may even realize that finding whichever name can be difficult, unless it is a jumbled meaningless word. You may encounter many advices what to do or what not to do when you want to register a domain, but in reality, you don't have much choices.

The quest for an available domain name should start at one of the well-established domain name registrars as GoDaddy, Name.com, Domain.com, or at some reliable hosting companies as BlueHost or Hostgator *. The real price for a domain name is about $15 dollars per year, but sometimes you can get it for less for the first year or free if it is included in the hosting plan. Our suggestion (at this moment) is that you go with Hostgator (biizly.com/hostgator01) since you can easily establish your web presence there (Domain + Hosting + WordPress) at affordable rates.

When searching for a reasonable domain name at any of the above-mentioned providers, here are some realistic (not always the best) options at your disposal:

MAKE UP A WORD

This is probably the best option you have. Many successful online businesses have made up words as their domain names. Take for example Google, Tumblr, Pinterest, Etsy, Weebly, Zillow, and many others. Our domain Biizly is just another example in the list.

When you use a new word as your domain, just make sure it's short, easy to read, spell and remember, but it should also not imply to something inappropriate. Ideally, the newly coined name should indicate your offering like Weebly or Shopify do, for example.

If you struggle to coin your own word, you can use this handy tool for generating new words (biizly.com/tool).

COIN TWO (OR THREE) WORD PHRASE

The shorter the domain the better. Anyhow, while it is almost impossible to find an available single-word domain with a meaning, it is still possible to find a domain with two words, especially when one of the words is made up. There are many successful websites that use two words in their domain name like: Facebook.com, Kickstarter.com, Statcounter.com, Godady.com, SoundCloud.com, DropBox.com, Hostgator.com etc. If you struggle to find the perfect domain for your business even

---

* For recommending these services we receive affiliate commission, but you don't pay a higher price for the products. If you decide to make a purchase through these links we would be thankful and would consider it as your credit for our effort to serve you with high quality content.

with two words combo, you can try using a three-word phrase or go for a hyphenated domain name (a dash between words) like in coca-cola.com or mercedes-benz.com. However, long names and hyphens are not recommended for several reasons.

USE NUMBER(S) IN YOUR DOMAIN.

This is not (always) a recommended option because it's hard to verbally communicate your domain if it has numbers in it. Anyway, since the promotion of a web business mostly goes online and sometimes the numbers have some purposeful meaning for your business it's not always a bad idea to include numbers in the domain. Here are some examples 1800flowers.com, news24.com 99designs.com, 7-eleven.com and w3schools.com.

USE UNCOMMON EXTENSION

The most commonly used domain extensions (TLD) are .com, .net and .org. When you plan to start a website, or an online business, almost everyone will advise you to get the .com version, but that's easily said than done. (If your target audience resides in a specific country you should consider using the country's specific extension (us, co.uk, de, jp, ru, fr, es, eu, etc.).)

So, if you run out of options to get an attractive .com (or country's specific) domain you may decide to go with another extension. The extensions available nowadays are countless. You may start your consideration with .net, .org, .co, .us, .it, .ly, .be, .is, .ltd. Then you may look for extensions like .site, .info, .biz, .me, .tv. You may even buy domains that end in .accountant, .gift, .guru, .band, .shop, .deals, .travel and many, many more. These new, keyword extension domains, may seem a little bit odd today but they may get more attention and value in the future. Anyway, be extra careful with these options since the internet users are still used to the .com extension. They may get skeptical when they encounter unusual ending of a domain name.

Popular sites with uncommon domain extensions for example are: Zoom.us, Who.is, Scoop.it Twitch.tv.

BUY AN EXPIRING DOMAIN (DOMAIN NAME BACKORDER)

Many domain names are registered (taken) but are not in use. If the owner fails to renew the domain, it will again become available for registration. If nobody else wants that name you can easily buy it at any registrar but if an expiring domain is attractive for you, it may be attractive for others too and they could get it before you. It also happens that the domain name registrants automatically buy any expiring domain names that are considered valuable and wanted. Backordering a domain means using a backordering service to acquire an expired domain as soon as it becomes available. To increase the chances to get a desired domain name you can use more than one backordering service.

At this link (biizly.com/db) you can find some details on backordering domain names.

Backordering a domain name is a good option since you could find an attractive name at a fair price. The negative thing is that there is no guarantee that you will get the domain, so you need to opt for more names in order to increase the chances of getting one. If there are other interested buyers, the backordering service will place the domain(s) into an auction where the price can go high. Another negative thing is that you can't buy an expiring domain right away. You need to wait for it to expire. Anyway, since finding a good domain is hard, it might be worth waiting.

BUY AN EXISTING DOMAIN

When you search for a domain name you may find out that some of your desired names are taken but on sale. Depending on the attractiveness of the domain, the prices may range from $50 up to thousands or even tens of thousands of dollars. If you have a nice budget for a domain and you encounter a perfect domain for your business within that budget, go for it.

GET HELP

If you find the process of finding decent domain name for your online business overwhelming, ask for help. Actually, you can go on Fiverr and starting from $5 you can get some suggestions. You can also place a contest for $10+ on freelancer for the same purpose and choose from several suggested names you will get.

Summary:

- Finding a good domain is hard, but there are still some available options.
- To (closely) match your business name with the domain name, register a domain first (even if you decide to register a company right away).
- To start a business online you don't need to register a company (soon), so now focus on your domain name.
- The best option for a domain name is to make up your own word and use the ".com" extension.
- Since it's hard to find a good domain name take some time, invest resources and/or find help.
- To simplify the process of starting a business online we suggest that you get a domain and a hosting plan at the same provider.

Task:

- Get a domain name + hosting plan at biizly.com/hostgator01 (Take some time)

In-depth readings (Search at Biizly.com):

Assessment: Identify Your Entrepreneurial Personality Type

9 ways to know if you have a great business idea

Porter's Model of Generic Strategies for Competitive Advantage

3.2. Website Builder (and a Hosting Plan) for Your Business Website

"What separates design from art is that design is meant to be ... functional"

– Cameron Moll

At a Glance:

A website to operate needs (1) Domain name, (2) Hosting, (3) Website system.

Available Website Builders / Management Systems (WMS).

WordPress as a website builder and its features.

Installing WordPress.

Establishing your online presence is the first tangible step of your online business journey. Building a website nowadays can be very easy with the modern and affordable **website builders** otherwise known as Website Management Systems (WMS)

If you want to get online, you have to take care of **the three basic elements of a functional website** that include: **1) domain name, 2) hosting plan** and **3) a website management system (WMS)**. A Website Management System (WMS), or simply Website System, is a software that will help you build and manage your website, a website hosting is a place on a server (computer), where your website (and the website system) will reside. The domain name is the address that will lead the visitors to your website.

You could arrange (get) all these three important elements in a bundle, but foremost you should reserve (purchase) your domain name since it can take a lot of time and energy. Taking care of the website system and the hosting plan afterwards is much simpler. Usually the hosting providers let you register a free domain name if you purchase a hosting plan too.

POPULAR WEBSITE SYSTEMS / BUILDERS

The modern website systems like WordPress, Joomla, Drupal, Blogger, Weebly, Wix, Shopify, Magento, Moodle etc., are more or less intuitive, user friendly, customizable, expandable, affordable, safe and so on. In other words, these systems could help any regular internet user to create an appealing website according to his/her business needs. All these systems (and many others) can help you build a website, but they may significantly differ in their core purpose, features and associated costs. For example, Shopify and Magento are specialized as online shops while Moodle is an e-learning platform.

The costs when using the above-mentioned web systems may vary from $0 to $30 or more, but you need to plan at least $5 a month if you want to get a domain name, decent performance and features for your website. Regarding the system you choose, there will be a need (or no need) for a separate hosting plan. Namely, Weebly and Shopify go together with hosting and cost $12 (with domain) and $29 per month respectively. WordPress, Joomla, and Magento are free open source systems but you would need a reliable hosting plan (self-hosted) that could start from $5 or up. Blogger is hosted (no need for a hosting plan) and free platform but is least customizable then the other available options and is mainly used for blogging.

WORDPRESS AND IT'S FEATURES

As we have mentioned several times before, we suggest you use WordPress together with an appropriate hosting plan for your online business website. There are more than few reasons why we warmly suggest WordPress (WP). First of all, WordPress is advanced, user-friendly website system that, at the same time, is open source and free. WordPress is the most widely used tool to build websites worldwide and has a large support community, wide selection of themes, widgets, plugins, regular updates etc.

You can use WordPress to build different online business models like informative websites (blog, news, magazine), online services, online shop, classified ads, social network and more. You can even find affordable WP developers to create a custom features/plugins for a unique online business you may have in mind, based on the

WordPress platform. (Don't confuse WordPress.org as self-hosted WMS with WordPress.com that is hosted blogging platform based on the WordPress website system)

Within the last several years, WordPress become more and more user-friendly and more easily manageable by regular internet users. You don't need technical knowledge (nor HTML or PHP) in order to set, arrange and manage your website. Anyhow, some other website systems like Wix, Weebly and Shopify may be simpler to use especially if you want a plug and play online store, like one, for example, you will get if you go with Shopify. These systems, that come with a monthly plan, will also have 24-hour support what is not the case with the free WordPress option. If you encounter a problem with WordPress you would need to rely on Google search, community support, video tutorials or affordable help from freelancers, what is not a bad option at all, especially if you are really dedicated to your online business.

Another reason we suggest you use WordPress is that the instructions that follow in this Guide, the next section and in Step 5, Building and Managing a Website, are mainly based on WordPress and its features. It doesn't mean you can't follow the Guide If you decide to use another system but choosing WordPress will simplify your journey.

HOSTING PLAN

As mentioned above, if you decide to go with open source website systems like WordPress, Joomla, Drupal Magento or Moodle you would need a reliable hosting plan. Most of the hosting providers out there, included the plans, enable one-click installation of these website systems at no additional cost.

If you followed our suggesting in the previous section, you possibly got a domain with a hosting plan where you can easily install WordPress in one click. If not, you could go at biizly.com/hostgator01, where you can get the domain + hosting * since you will need them for the next steps.

If you already have purchased only a domain name here are some options for a hosting plan: at HostGator (biizly.com/h36) or at BlueHost (biizly.com/h1)* both with one-click WordPress option. When purchasing domain name and a hosting plan on

---

* For recommending these services we receive affiliate commission, but you don't pay a higher price for the products. If you purchase a hosting plan through our links feel free to ask for some help and directions.

different providers you will need to set the DNS addresses at your domain name provider to point to your hosting plan. This is why we recommend you get them at the same provider in a bundle.

If you decide to go with another open source system than WordPress, you can also use the above-suggested hosting options

INSTALLING WORDPRESS

Once you have a domain and a hosting plan you can easily install WordPress, (or any other open source system).

In Hostgator and other hosting providers that use cPanel you should look for a button like this one:

where you could follow the simple instructions.

(cPanel is a web hosting control panel and you will get link, username and password to login there after you purchase the hosting plan. Keep these in a handy and safe place)

Alternatively, regarding the hosting provider you have chosen, in order to finish the installation of WordPress watch the appropriate video tutorial (links below) to install WordPress. As you can see in the videos, the process is really simple. Prior to the installation you will need to login to the hosting panel using the username and password.

Installing WordPress at Hostgator (biizly.com/wph)

Installing WordPress at BlueHost (biizly.com/wpb)

Installing WordPress at Godaddy (biizly.com/wpg)

If you used different hosting provider, search for tutorials at Google using the search term "Installing WordPress at <<YourHostingProvider>>". If your hosting provider does not support one click installation of WordPress you should download the WP package at WordPress.org, upload it to your hosing using file manager or FTP software and them manually install it.

When you finally get your WordPress website installed, you can follow the link http://yourdomain.com/login *(change yourdomain.com to your real domain name)* to log in to the dashboard of your site.

The login interface to your WordPress website will look like this:

To login to your site's dashboard you will need to use the admin username and password acquired during the WordPress installation process, different from the cPanel platform (also keep them in a handy and safe place).

(You might need to wait up to 24 hours after the purchase of the domain in order to access your website since the DNS addresses need to update worldwide.)

Now you are fully prepared to finally go online. Your WordPress site is now functional, but you need to do some initial adjustments and to add some content before you announce the official start of your online business.

Summary:

- Modern WMS are intuitive, user friendly, customizable, expandable, affordable, safe.
- Depending on your preferences and goals you can choose from a wide selection of website management systems (WMS) in order to build your website.
- We suggest to use WordPress with a reliable hosting plan (This guide is mostly focused on WordPress website)

- WordPress, Joomla, Magento, Moodle, are free, open source systems and additionally require a reliable hosting plan that would cost at least $5 per month.
- Weebly and Shopify come together with hosting, could be easier to operate but cost at least $12/$29 per month.
- Blogger is self-hosted blogging platform that is free and reliable but with limited customizability.
- To avoid the trouble of setting DNS addresses manually get a domain and hosting at one provider where you can install WordPress in a very simple process.

Task:

- Install WordPress on your hosting plan (first get a domain + hoisting at biizly.com/hostgator01)

3.3. Initial Website Build and First Outreach

"You Never Get a Second Chance to Make a First Impression." – Will Rogers

At a Glance:

Reasons to establish your initial web presence fast.

Initial website adjustments.

Initial contents to create

Initial outreach for partners and (potential) customer

As soon as you get your domain name (and the hosting plan) you should start working to put your initial website online. The initial website would not be a fully functional site representing your business idea but is a good starting point from where you can build your online business, step by step. Such website would not have all the features of your business idea

(or the products) but could explain the reasoning behind it to the very first visitors.

There might be several motives why you would like to establish your initial web presence fast. First of all, making a simple website is a no-brainer and **can be done even in 1 hour** or less. Other thing is that, at this stage of your online business journey you may want to **contact potential business partners**, co-founders, team members, employees, investors and so on. You may even want to test the reactions of the first potential customers in order to **validate your business idea** (with a landing page). To earn the trust of some (or all) above-mentioned stakeholders, you should create a neat initial website, addressing to their points of interest.

Communicating your business idea, or your offering, would be much easier if you have a ready website and a business card where you will put the web address too.

Another important reason to build an initial website is to start with the marketing as soon as possible. It is never too early to start the online marketing effort. It might be too early for advertising though, especially if your site is not fully functional, but there are many other free online marketing activities you can undertake at this point. If you expect any visitors/potential clients at this stage, you may also want to start building your subscribers list.

So, if you have purchased a domain and hosting (in the previous section) and you don't want your website to read "under construction" follow the link http://<<yourdomain.com>>/login/ to log into the dashboard of your site (see the image below) and start putting the pieces together.

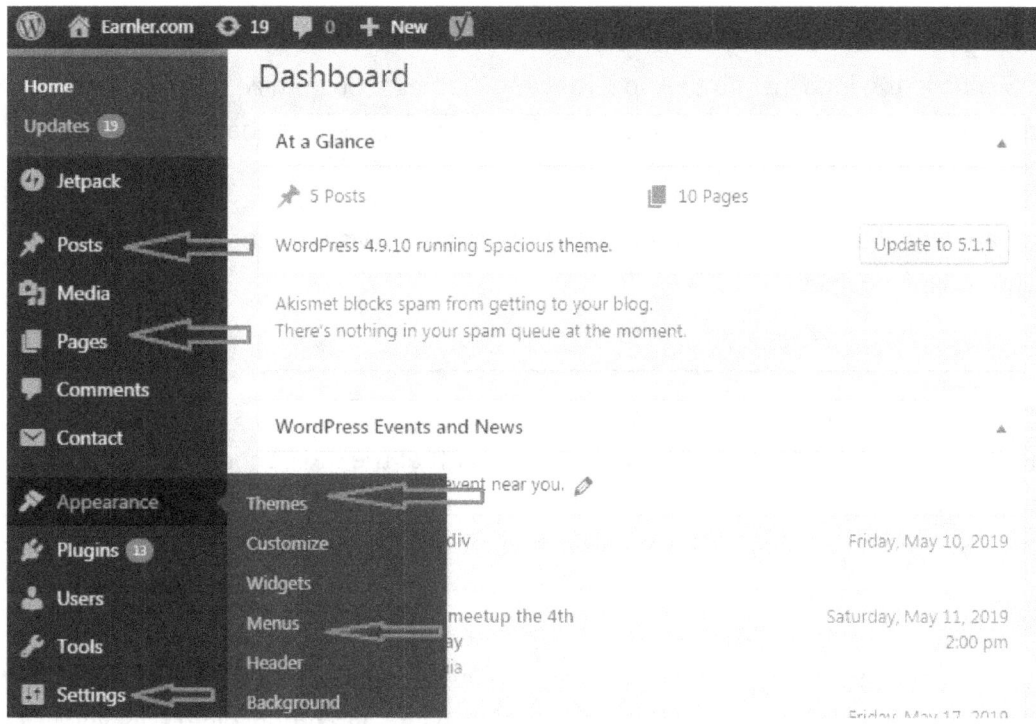

Below in this guide you will find a list, short descriptions and video tutorials of all elements/tasks you should put together in order to establish your initial online presence.

INITIAL WEBSITE ADJUSTMENTS

Theme.

There is a wide selection of free WordPress themes (website appearances) you can use. To set a theme, while at the dashboard (see image above), go to Appearance > Themes > Ad New. You can search themes by categories, features, layout and keywords. (After you install the theme, you will need to activate it.) Since there is a huge number of themes available, to save you some precious time, we would suggest you use the Spacious theme by ThemeGrill. This theme is free, simple, easy to setup and appropriate for different use cases. If you need to, you can always change the theme later. (Watch Video how to change the Theme at biizly.com/wp1)

Logo.

Adding a logo to a WordPress site is a piece of cake. First you need to create a logo yourself or engage a freelancer to do it for you. (Search Google for: *Create a free logo online*)

After you have the logo just go to Appearance > Themes > Customize > Site identity, where you can add the logo and switch on/off the textual title and the tagline of the site. (Watch Video at biizly.com/wp2)

Having an appealing logo is very important since it gives a visual identity of your site and your online business.

Permalinks structure

On the dashboard go to Settings > Permalinks and change common settings to Post Name. You can use another structure but remember that the URLs should be as short as possible and readable by the users. You should also now that once you choose the structure you shouldn't change it ever. (Watch Video at biizly.com/wp3)

Google Search Console

If you want your site to be noticed by Google, the most important search engine, you should register it at the Google Search Console. Google Search Console tracks your website performance in Google search, but it also speeds the indexing of your pages so that they can appear in the search results. Appearing in the search results is very important since it can bring many potential customers to your website.

Plugins

The plugins can enhance the appearance and the performance of your site and they can also add new features to the basic WordPress installation. You can use plugins to fight spam, improve loading speed, add sliders, integrate ads, create e-shop and so on. At this point, you could need plugins for statistics, sitemaps, home page builder, and contact form. You will install other plugins later if you need them. To install plugins, go to Plugins > Ad New (Use the search form to find the plugins we suggest below). After you install you need to activate the plugins in order to use them. Some plugins would need some setting up to function properly.

Web statistics

Since you go online you would probably want to know if any visitors come to your website. The simplest way to track your early visitors is to install the WP Power Stats plugin. Later (in Step 7) you will learn how to use Google Analytics to track the behavior of your site visitors and the site performance in details.

Sitemaps

If you want your site to be indexed fast and properly by Google and the other search engines you should have sitemaps. A plugin like Google XML Sitemaps will help you automatically generate sitemap every time a new page or post is added to the site. Any time a new sitemap is generated by Google XML Sitemaps it is also submitted to the Google Search Console.

INITIAL CONTENT

The content is king, as you may know. You will have to continuously enrich your site with interesting and engaging content if you want to attract, retain visitors and turn them into (loyal) customers. At this phase, you should put at least come content that will make you appear as legitimate web business.

Homepage

The homepage of your website should represent the most important aspects of your business. If your website is an informative one at your homepage should be the most appealing content (posts, news, videos etc). If you sell products you should put the bestsellers and/or the current promotions there. I you offer personal or business services you should emphasize your competences (principles of work, portfolio, references, testimonials, etc.). If you offer software, you should present the features and the prices with an option for a trial.

There are two basic options for your home page when you use WordPress. (To select, go to Settings > Reading > Your homepage displays.) The first option is to set your latest posts to appear at your home page. The other option is to set a specific page to be your homepage. To do the later you need to create the page first (Pages > Ad New or + New > Page). To get the best out of this option you could use plugin like Elemntor that can help you add elements and edit the homepage with ease. The elements may include but are not limited to sliders, galleries, statements, post carousel, testimonials, features, products, videos etc.

About us/Team

While your homepage mainly presents your offering, the About page will explain who is behind the website or what is the main idea of your business. Not all visitors go to the about page but those who go there really care. By presenting your business in the best light you can earn their trust.

FAQ

The Frequently Asked Question is usually a very useful page that can help the first-time visitors navigate and use your site, understand your business concept, learn about your offering and so on. FAQs work the best if they come from real visitors of your site but you can start form your guesses, what they may ask, of form the questions you got while you presented the business idea to your friends.

Contact page/ Location

Regardless of your business type you should always have contact information and a contact form on your website. This is not only for potential business partners and interested customers to contact you, but also to give more credibility to your online business. If you have phone number, physical address (location) and other options for a contact you will appear as a real and credible business. To add a contact form on the contact page you will have to install a plugin as Contact Form 7

Products/Services

A website is an excellent place to present your products and services even if you have only brick and mortar business. At your homepage you may present only part of your offering and in less details. Separate page(s) for your products and services will give you more freedom to present and explain the details. If your products are not ready yet you can just announce them or even offer presales. Besides the pages for your products and services you may add pages for your portfolio, references and/or testimonials in order to increase your credibility.

Blog posts/Articles/News

Regardless of your online business model, it is highly recommended that you have a blog that will accompany the site's main content and offering. Especially, with the informative website business model your blog posts/articles will be the main offering. Creating attractive posts on a regular basis will help you bring visitors to your site and earn revenue. While the pages (described above) directly represent/explain your offering or business, the blog posts can give closely or distantly related information that might be of interest to your customers. Other difference between pages and post in the light of the WP platform is that post have time stamp, author, categories and tags what is not the case with the pages. For now, create at least 5 posts in order to create a better user experience for your initial visitors. To create post, go to Posts > Ad New or + New > Post. (Watch video at biizly.com/wp4)

Main Menu

(Editing the main menu is a website adjustment, not content, but since you needed some initial content to link to, we placed it at the end)

The Main Menu or the Primary Menu is usually located at the very top of the site or just beneath the site's logo and/or the header. Since the Main menu is very important for the site's navigation and understanding of the content, you should put links at least to the following pages: Home, About, Products/Services, Blog, Contact/Location. If you site has some important specifics put them too, like we put a Start Here link at Biizly.com. To create and edit menus go to Appearance > Menus. (Watch video at biizly.com/wp5)

(Detailed management of a WordPress website will be presented in Step 5.)

INITIAL OUTREACH

Now that you have your initial website ready you can start with the marketing activities. It is never too early to **start promoting**, especially now when you have something to show off. Before you fully develop your offering and the website you can set a solid foundation for your future marketing activities. (Something we will discuss in more details in Step 6.)

First thing you could do is to create a **business cards** that represent you online business and you as a founder. For most of the web business models a business card wouldn't be much of a use but is nice to have one. The business cards could be very handy if you go to expos, conferences or if you approach potential partners and/or customers, especially if you target businesses as customers.

Another important thing to do now is to **create business profiles/pages at Facebook, Twitter and Pinterest**. If you find it appropriate and if you have the time, you can also create profiles at Instagram and Tumblr. Make sure you place the links of the social media profiles you have created on your website at prominent locations as header, sidebar, at the contact page and in the footer. Also, don't forget to share your previously created pages and posts on the social media profiles you have created for your business but on your personal profiles too.

Summary:

- There are several reasons why you would need to set up your website fast.
- With the initial site you can; approach partners, validate your business idea, start the marketing, start building your members list etc.
- Developing an initial website in WordPress is simple and easy (follow our simple directions)
- To finally establish your online presence (after you install the website system - WordPress or other), you should at least do some initial website adjustments, create initial content and create social media profiles for your business.
- Initial website adjustments: Theme, Logo, Initial settings, Plugins, etc.)
- Initial content: Homepage, Products/Services, Blog posts, Contact, About etc.
- Initial outreach:
  - o Create a business card
  - o Create business profiles at Facebook, Twitter, Pinterest, Instagram
  - o Share information and post on all profiles, including the personal

Tasks:

- Do the initial website adjustments (Theme, Logo, Permalinks, Google Search Console, Plugins, Web statistics, Sitemaps, Main Menu.)
- Create initial content (Homepage, About, FAQ, Contact, Products/Services)
- Create/Write at least 5 Blog posts
- Create business profiles/pages at Facebook, Twitter and Pinterest.

In-Depth Readings (Search at Biizly.com):
Exploring the WordPress Dashboard
11 Tips for Your Initial Website Build
The Magic to Writing Your Initial Website Content Exposed
How to Set Up Your Social Media Profiles

What's Next?

Now that you have a ready website, promising business idea and an outlined business concept you are prepared to take your business to the next level. First, setup your back-office operations: team up, allocate and outsource tasks, set offices (if needed), integrate the revenue model, accept payments, manage inventory etc. (Step 4), then take full care of your website (Step 5) and undertake promotional activities (Step 6).

Everything you need to know for the following steps could be found in our **Online Business Startup Guide – Part 2** (Coming Soon)**:**

> Step 4: Back Office Operations for Your Online Business
>
> Step 5: Building and Managing a Website
>
> Step 6: Online Marketing (Attracting Online Visitors and Clients)

You could subscribe at the Biizly.com in order to be notified when the part 2 is coming out.

Biizly.com

Online Business Startup Guide
info@biizly.com
https://Biizly.com